BENEDICTUS DE SPINOZA.
Cui natura, Deus, rerum cui cognitus ordo,
Hoc Spinofa ftatu confpiciendus erat.
Expreffere viri faciem, fed pingere mentem
Zeuxidis artifices non valuere manus.
Illa viget fcriptis: illic fublimia tractat:
Hunc quicunque cupis nofcere, fcripta lege.

After an Engraving by a Contemporary.

SPINOZA'S SHORT TREATISE

ON

GOD, MAN AND HUMAN WELFARE

TRANSLATED FROM THE DUTCH BY
LYDIA GILLINGHAM ROBINSON

CHICAGO
THE OPEN COURT PUBLISHING CO.
LONDON AGENTS
KEGAN PAUL, TRENCH, TRÜBNER & CO., LTD.
1909

BENEDICTUS DE SPINOZA

Inscription Under His Portrait

Cui natura, Deus rerum cui cognitus ordo,
  Hoc Spinosa statu conspiciendus erat.
Expressere viri faciem, sed pingere mentem
  Zeuxidiis artifices non valuere manus.
Illa viget scriptis: illic sublimia tractat:
  Hunc quicunque cupis noscere scripta lege.

* * *

Dit is de schaduw van Spinoza's zienlijk beelt,
Daar't gladde koper geen sieraat aan kon geven;
Maar zijn gezegent brein, zoo rijk hem meégedeelt,
Doet in zijn schriften hem aanschouwen naar het leven.
Wie oil begeerte tot de wysheit heest gehad,
Hier was die Zuiver en op't snedigste gevat.

* * *

He to whom Nature and God were known, and the cosmical order
  Here he, Spinoza, is seen; here are his features portrayed;
But the man's face has been pictured alone. As for painting his spirit,
  Verily Zeuxides' hands would not suffice for the task.
Seek in his writings his mind, where he treateth of things that are
    lofty.
  He who is anxious to know, therefore, his writings must read.

iii

TABLE OF CONTENTS

APPENDIX

TRANSLATOR'S PREFACE

This *Short Treatise on God, Man and Human Welfare* (commonly referred to with the abbreviated title, " Short Treatise ") was Spinoza's first philosophical work. The exact date of its authorship is not known, but it is probable that he wrote it between the ages of 25 and 30. He was early surrounded by a coterie of friends who looked to him for their guidance in philosophical matters, and when in 1660, at the age of 28, he left Amsterdam for the vicinity of Leyden, it is thought that he either left this Treatise behind him to be circulated among his friends, or sent it back to them soon after his departure. It was originally written in Latin, but was soon translated into Dutch by one of his friends. Both Latin and Dutch versions were lost sight of until the middle of the nineteenth century when Dutch manuscripts were discovered, but no Latin original has ever been found.

The latest and best edition of the Dutch is that of J. Van Vloten and J. P. N. Land in Volume III of their *Benedicti de Spinoza Opera*.[1] This gives the most authentic manuscript entire with occasional pertinent variants from the other in brackets and footnotes. It is from this text that the present English translation has been made. Where a vari-

[1] The Hague, 1895.

ant manuscript reading has there been indicated, that alternative which seemed the simplest and most natural has been adopted without explanation or apology. For more particular items of textual criticism the student must still have recourse to Van Vloten and Land's edition.

The many long and unsigned footnotes are those of the Dutch manuscript as given in the same edition, and are evidently in part Spinoza's own and partly from the hand of the Dutch translator. Where Latin terms appear in the Dutch edition either in the text or parenthetically, they are faithfully retained in the hope that some at least may be quotations from Spinoza's own manuscript.

As early as 1867 Professor C. Schaarschmidt of Bonn translated the Short Treatise into German as Vol. 91 of Dürr's *Philosophische Bibliothek,* and this has been widely used by those unacquainted with the Dutch language. Within the last year a new edition of this work has appeared which besides being greatly improved typographically bears evidence also of text revision, while its practical value is enhanced by an index. There is another German translation by Sigwart and also a French version made by Janet.

It is a remarkable fact that no English translation has been made hitherto, for the Treatise is of too great value to the student of Spinoza and philosophy in general to be ignored. In small compass it foreshadows some of the most important themes of the Ethics, and expresses them in a less pretentious and simpler method. It is most important therefore that the student of Spinoza's philosophy should familiarize himself with this Short Treatise as a preparation for the right comprehension of the larger work.

Spinoza's literary style is often loose and indefinite. The translator has purposely refrained from substituting repetitions for the many indefinite terms of reference used throughout, lest the effort to make a clearer and more readable English would result in so far in an interpretation rather than Spinoza's own unadorned statement. Thus his style has been retained with all its ambiguities and even crudities where they occur, so that the reader will have as faithful a reproduction of Spinoza's Short Treatise as is possible with the material at hand, and is therefore at liberty to form his own opinion with regard to its merits and intent.

* * *

No other philosopher has been so variously judged and misjudged as Spinoza. Opinions have differed in all conceivable shades and his system has been credited with being anything from the most theistic mysticism to a gross materialism which it was claimed he was too cowardly to admit. Some give no heed to his definitions but argue that because he makes frequent use of the familiar religious terms, such as "God," he must have the same anthropomorphic conception of God as they themselves; others note the definitions, and because these differ from their own preconceptions, they say, "Behold the Atheist!"

The Short Treatise discusses the same subjects as the Ethics and from the same point of view; but whereas the latter is a matured and carefully elaborated system of thought, its laborious adhesion to Descartes's ponderous mathematical method in vogue at the time, seems to have eliminated the personal equation which is by no means without value. On the other hand the more informal character of the little Treatise makes it possible to gain an insight into the young philosopher's efforts to grasp at a tangible support upon which his highest intellectual and moral aspirations might rest after he had lost faith in the reality of the symbols of his childhood.

Had he written solely for the instruction of others, he would have done better to have told " What God is " before he undertook to prove " That God is." By considering his definition first, the reader would at once grasp his point of view and not labor under the delusion that Spinoza is proving the existence of whatever conception of God the reader may chance to hold. Instead he would realize that though Spinoza lived in the seventeenth century his God (which in the Ethics is made identical with the metaphysical term " substance ") is not far removed from the " God of evolution " of to-day; that he is the perfect cause of all things, but that it would be contrary to his perfection if he could avoid doing what he has done or causing what he has caused; and that therefore some attributes which are usually ascribed to him, but which properly belong to man (love, compassion and also will), are but " modes "

which cannot exist without the substances of which
they are modes, and so can not be attributed to a
being whose existence depends on nothing outside
of himself.

L. G. R.

LA SALLE, ILLINOIS, June 15, 1908.

SPINOZA AND HIS METAPHYSICS [1]

BY DR. ALBERT SCHWEGLER

Baruch Spinoza was born in Amsterdam on the 24th of November 1632. His parents, Jews of Portuguese extraction, were well-to-do tradespeople, and gave him the education of a scholar. He studied with diligence the Bible and the Talmud. He soon exchanged, however, the study of theology for that of physics and the works of Descartes. About the same time, having long broken inwardly with Judaism, he broke with it outwardly also, without, however, formally embracing Christianity. In order to escape the persecutions of the Jews, who had excommunicated him, and with whom his life was in danger, he left Amsterdam and betook himself to Rhynsburg, near Leyden, but settled finally at the Hague, where, wholly absorbed in scientific pursuits, he lived in the greatest seclusion. He earned his living by the polishing of optical glasses, which

---

[1] Translated from the German by James Hutchinson Stirling. The entire chapter on Spinoza is taken intact from Schwegler's *History of Philosophy* (Eng. version, Edinburgh; Edmonston & Co., 1879), with the single exception of the last paragraph which gives the author's own valuation of Spinoza's system and is here avoided as savoring rather too much of an interpretation.

his friends disposed of.   The Elector of the Palat-
inate, Carl Ludwig, made him an offer of a philosophical chair at Heidelberg, with the promise of
complete liberty of opinion; but Spinoza declined
it.   Delicate by nature, suffering from ill-health for
years, Spinoza died of consumption on the 21st of
February 1677, at the early age of forty-four.   The
cloudless purity and sublime tranquillity of a perfectly wise man were mirrored in his life.   Ab-
stemious, satisfied with little, master of his passions, never immoderately sad or glad, gentle and
benevolent, of a character admirably pure, he faithfully followed the doctrines of his philosophy, even
in his daily life.   His chief work, the *Ethics,* was
published the year he died.   He would have liked
probably to have published it in his lifetime, but the
hateful name of Atheist must have deterred him.
His most intimate friend, Ludwig Mayer, a physi-
cian, in accordance with his will, superintended the
publication after his death.

The system of Spinoza is supported on three fundamental notions, from which all the others follow
with mathematical necessity.   These notions are
those of substance, attribute, and mode.

(*a*) Spinoza starts from the Cartesian definition
of substance: substance is that which, for its existence, stands in need of nothing else.   This notion
of substance being assumed, there can exist, according to Spinoza, only a single substance.   What
is through its own self alone is necessarily infinite,
unconditioned and unlimited by anything else.

Spontaneous existence is the absolute power to exist,)
which cannot depend on anything else, or find in anything else a limit, a negation of itself; only unlimited
being is self-subsistent, substantial being.   A plurality of infinites, however, is impossible; for one
were indistinguishable from the other.   A plurality
of substances, as assumed by Descartes, is necessarily,
therefore, a contradiction.   It is possible for only
one substance, and that an absolutely infinite substance, to exist.   The given, finite reality necessarily
presupposes such single, self-existent substance.   It
were a contradiction, that only the finite, not the
infinite, should have existence; that there should
be only what is conditional and caused by something else, and not also what is self-existent and self-
subsistent.   The absolute substance is rather the |
real cause of all and every existence; it alone is '
actual, unconditioned being; it is the sole virtue
of existence, and through this virtue everything
finite is: without it there is nothing, with it there is
all; all reality is comprehended in it, as, beside it,
self-dependent being there is none; it is not only
cause of all being, but it is itself all being; every
special existence is only a modification (individuali-
zation), of the universal substance itself, which, by
force of inner necessity, expands its own infinite
reality into an immeasurable quantity of being, and
comprises within itself every possible form of existence.   This one substance is named by Spinoza)
God.   As is self-evident, then, we must leave out '
of view here the Christian idea of God, the con-

ception of an individual, spiritual personality.
Spinoza expressly declares that he entertains quite
a different idea of God from Christians; he distinctly maintains that all existence, material existence included, springs directly from God as the single substance; and he laughs at those who see in
the world aught but an accident of the divine substance itself. He recognizes in the views of these
a dualism which would annul the necessary unity of
all things — a self-substantiation of the world,
which would destroy the sole causality of God.
The world is for him no product of the divine will
that stands *beside* God, free: it is an emanation
of the creative being of God, which being is, by
its very nature, infinite. God to Spinoza, is only
the substance of things, and not anything else. The
propositions, that there is only one God, and that
the substance of all things is only one, are to him
identical.

What properly is substance now? What is its
positive nature? We have here a question that
from the position of Spinoza is very hard to answer.
Partly for this reason, that a definition, according
to Spinoza, must include the proximate cause (be
genetic) of what is to be defined, whilst substance,
as increate, can have no cause external to itself.
Partly, again, and chiefly for this reason, that to
Spinoza, all determination is negation (*omnis de-
terminatio est negatio*, though only an incidental
expression, is the fundamental idea of the entire
system), for determination implies a defect of ex-

istence, a relative non-being. Special positive desig-
nations, then, would only reduce substance to something finite. Declarations in its regard, consequently, must be only negative and provisory, as, for
example, it has no external cause, is not a many, cannot possibly be divided, etc. Spinoza is reluctant
to say even that it is one, because this predicate
may be easily taken as numerical, and then it might
appear as if another, the many, were opposed to it.
Thus there are left only such positive expressions
as enunciate its absolute relation to its own self.
It is in this sense that Spinoza says of it, it is the
cause of itself, or its nature implies existence. And
it is only another expression for the same thought
when he calls substance eternal, for by eternity he
understands existence itself, so far as it is conceived
as following from the definition of the object, in
the same sense in which geometricians speak of the
eternal qualities of figures. Spinoza applies to substance the predicate infinite also, so far as the notion of infinitude is identical to him with the notion
of true being, with the absolute affirmation of existence. In the same manner the allegation, that God
is free, expresses only what the others express, to
wit, negatively, that all external force is excluded,
and positively, that God is in agreement with himself, that his being corresponds to the laws of his
nature.

In sum, there is only one infinite substance, ex-
cludent of all determination and negation from itself, the one being in every being — God.

(*b*) Besides infinite substance or God, Descartes had assumed two derivative and created substances, the one spirit or thought, the other matter or extension. These also re-appear here as the two ground-forms under which Spinoza subsumes all reality — the two " attributes " in which the single substance reveals itself to us, so far as it is the cause of all that is. How now — this is the perplexing question, the Achilles' heel of the Spinozistic system — are these attributes related to the infinite substance? Substance cannot wholly disappear in them; else it were determinate, limited, and in contradiction, therefore, to its own notion. If then these attributes do not exhaust the objective being of substance, it follows that they are determinations in which substance takes form for the subjective apprehension of understanding; or for behoof of understanding all is once for all divided into thought and extension. And this is the conception of Spinoza. An attribute is for him what understanding perceives in substance as constitutive of its nature. The two attributes are therefore determinations, which express the nature of substance in these precise forms, only for perception. Substance itself being unexhausted by any such specialties of form, the attributes must be conceived as but expressions of its nature for an understanding that is placed apart from it. That such understanding should perceive substance only under these precise two forms is indifferent to substance itself, which *impliciter* possesses an infinitude of attributes. That

is to say, all possible attributes, not limitations, may
be assumed for substance. It is only the human
understanding that invests substance with the two
specially mentioned, and exclusively with these two,
for of all the notions of the understanding, they are
the only ones actually positive or expressive of reality. To the understanding substance is thought,
then, considered under the attribute of thought,
and extension, considered under the attribute of
extension. In a word, the two attributes are but
empirically derived determinations, that are incom-
mensurate besides with the nature of substance.
Substance stands behind them as the absolute infinite which cannot be comprehended in any such
special notions. The attributes explain not what
substance really is; and in its regard consequently
appear contingent. Spinoza fails to supply any
principle of union between the notion of absolute
substance and the particular manner in which it
manifests itself in the two attributes.

In their own natural relation, the attributes, as
with Descartes, are to be directly opposed to each
other. They are attributes of one and the same substance, it is true, but each is independent in itself,
as independent, indeed, as the very substance which
it is supposed *realiter* to represent. Between
thought and extension, then, spirit and matter, there
can be no mutual influence; what is material can
only have material causes, what is spiritual only
spiritual ones, as ideas, volition, etc. Neither spirit,
consequently, can act on matter, nor matter on spirit.

xx   SPINOZA'S SHORT TREATISE

Thus far, then, Spinoza adheres to the Cartesian severance of spirit and matter. But, as referred to the notion of the single substance, both worlds are equally again one and the same; there is a perfect agreement between them, a thorough parallelism. One and the same substance is thought as present in both attributes — one and the same substance in the various forms of existence under either. "The idea of the circle and the actual circle are the same thing, now under the attribute of thought and again under that of extension." From the one substance there proceeds, in effect, only a single infinite series of things, but a series of things in a variety of forms, even after subjection primarily to one or other of the forms of the attributes. The various things exist, like substance itself, as well under the ideal form of thought, as under the real form of extension. For every spiritual form there is a correspondent corporeal one, as for every corporeal form a correspondent spiritual one. Nature and spirit are different, indeed, but they are not isolatedly apart: they are everywhere together, like type and antitype, like things and the ideas of things, like object and subject, in which last the object mirrors itself, or what *realiter* is, *idealiter* reflects itself. The world were not the product of a single substance, if these two elements, thought and extension, were not, at every point in inseparable identity, united in it. Spinoza subjects, in particular, the relation between body and soul to the idea of this inseparable unity of spirit and matter,

a unity which, according to him, pervades the whole
of nature, but in various grades of perfection. And
here we have his simple solution of the problem,
which, from the point of view of Descartes, was so
difficult, and even inexplicable. In man, as everywhere else, extension and thought (the latter, in
his case, not only as feeling and perception, but as
self-conscious reason) are together and inseparable.
The soul is the consciousness that has for its objects the associated body, and through the inter-
vention of the body, the remaining corporeal world,
so far as it affects the body; the body is the real
organism whose states and affections consciously re-
flect themselves in the soul. But any influence of
the one on the other does not for this very reason
exist; soul and body are the same thing, but expressed in the one case only as conscious thought,
in the other as material extension. They differ
only in form, so far as the nature and life of the
body, so far, that is, as the various corporeal im-
pressions, movements, functions, which obey wholly
and solely the laws of the material organism, spon-
taneously coalesce in the soul to the unity of consciousness, conception, thought.

(c) The special individual forms which are ideas
or material things, according as they are considered
under the attribute of thought or under the attribute
of extension, receive their explanation at the hands
of Spinoza by reference to the notion of accident,
or, as he names it, *modus*. By *modi* we are to understand, then, the various individual finite forms,

in which infinite substance particularizes itself.
The *modi* are to substance what the waves are to
the sea — shapes that perpetually die away, that
never are. Nothing finite is possessed of a self-
subsistent individuality. The finite individual
exists, indeed, because the unlimited productive
power of substance must give birth to an infinite
variety of particular finite forms; but it has no proper
reality — it exists only in substance. Finite things
are only the last, the most subordinate, the most
external terms of existence, in which the universal
life gives itself specific forms, and they bear the
stamp of finitude in that they are subjected, without will, without resistance, to the causal chain that
pervades this world. The divine substance is free
only in the inner essence of its own nature, but individual things are not free, they are a prey to all the
others with which they are connected. This is their
finitude, indeed, that they are conditioned and determined, not by themselves, but by what is alien to
them. They constitute the domain of pure necessity, within which each is free and independent only
so far as power has been given it by nature to assert itself against the rest, and maintain intact its
own existence and its proper and peculiar interests.

These are the fundamental notions, the fundamental features of the system of Spinoza. As for his
practical philosophy, it may be characterized in a
few words. Its main propositions follow of necessity
from the metaphysical principles which we have
just seen. And for first example we have the in-

admissibleness of what is called free-will. For, man being only modus, what is applicable to the others is applicable to him; he is involved in the infinite series of conditional causes; and free-will, therefore, cannot be predicated of him. His will, like every other bodily function, must be determined by *something*, whether an impression from without or an impulse from within. Men believe themselves free, simply because they are conscious of their own acts, but not of the motives of them. In the same way, the notions, which we usually connect with the words good and bad, rest on an error, as follows at once from the simple notion of the absolute divine cause. Good and bad are not anything actual in things themselves, but only express relative notions suggested to us by our own comparison of things one with another. We form for ourselves, namely, from the observation of particular things, a certain general conception, and this conception we continue to regard as if it were a necessary rule for all other particular things. Should now some single individual clash with our general conception, that individual would be regarded as imperfect, and as in disagreement with its own nature. Sin, then, the bad, is only relative, and not positive, for nothing happens contrary to the will of God. It is a mere negation or privation, and appears something positive only to our finite minds. There is no bad to God. What, then, are good and bad? That is good which is useful to us, that bad which prevents us from attaining to the good.

That, again, is useful which procures us greater reality, which preserves and promotes our being. Our true being, however, is reason; reason is the inner nature of our soul; it is reason that makes us free; for it is from reason that we possess the motive and the power to resist the molestations of things from without, to determine our own action according to the law of the due preservation and promotion of our existence, and to place ourselves as regards all things in a relation adequate to our nature. What, consequently, contributes to our knowledge, that alone is useful. But the highest knowledge is the knowledge of God. The highest virtue of the soul is to know and love God. From knowledge of God there arises for us the supreme happiness and joy, the bliss of the soul: it gives us peace in the thought of the eternal necessity of all things; it delivers us from all discord and discontent, from all fruitless struggling against the finitude of our own being; it raises us from life in sense to that life in intellect, which, freed from all the troubles and the trials of the perishable, is occupied only with itself and with the eternal. Felicity, then, is not the reward of virtue — it is virtue itself.

PART I

GOD

PREFACE TO THE DUTCH MANU-SCRIPT

Originally written by B. D. S. in the Latin tongue for the benefit of those of his disciples who wished to apply themselves to the practice of ethics and true philosophy, and now translated into the Dutch language for the benefit of the lovers of truth and virtue; in order that those who greatly boast that they put dirt and filth in the hands of the credulous in place of ambergris may once have their mouths stopped and cease to slander those things which they do not yet understand, namely, God, themselves, and to help provide for the welfare of each other; and also that the sick in understanding may recover by virtue of the spirit of meekness and forbearance after the pattern of the Lord Christ, our best Instructor.

CHAPTER I

THAT GOD IS

In regard to the first point, namely whether there is a God, we would say that first it can be proved *a priori* thus:

1. Everything which we clearly and distinctly understand to belong to the nature [1] of a thing, we can truly affirm also of the thing itself;

But that existence belongs to the nature of God we can clearly and distinctly understand;

Therefore, etc.

Or, in other words,

2. The essences of things exist from all eternity and will remain unchanged into all eternity.

The essence of God is existence; [2]

---

[1] Limited nature is meant, by virtue of which the thing is what it is, and which can in no way be separated from it without also at the same time destroying the thing; as for instance it belongs to the essence of a mountain to have a valley, or, the essence of a mountain is that it has a valley; which fact is indeed eternal and unchangeable and must always be in the concept of a mountain even though the mountain itself does not exist and never did.

[2] *De wezentlijkheid Gods is wezentheid.* This peculiar Dutch expression might be imitated in English etymologically by saying, " The essentiality of God is essence." — Tr.

Therefore, etc.

That God exists can be thus proved *a posteriori*:

If man has an idea of God then God must exist formally [8] (*formelijk*).

Now man has an idea of God;

Therefore, etc.

The first we prove as follows:

If there is an idea of God, then the cause of this idea must formally exist and must contain within itself all that the idea possesses objectively.

But there is an idea of God;

Therefore, etc.

In order to demonstrate the first part of this proof we will lay down the following principles, to-wit:

(1) That there is an infinite number of knowable things;

---

[8] From the definition given below in Chapter II ascribing to God infinite attributes, we can prove his existence thus: Everything that we see clearly and distinctly belongs to the nature of a thing, we can also truly affirm of the thing. But to the nature of a being that has infinite attributes there belongs one attribute, which is existence. Therefore, etc.— Now to say to this that it may well be affirmed of the idea but not of the thing itself, is false; for the idea does not consist materially (*materialiter*) of the attribute which belongs to this being; therefore that which is stated belongs neither to the object nor to that which is stated of the object; thus between the concept (*idea*) and the thing conceived (*ideatum*) there is a great difference, and therefore what is stated of the thing is not stated of the idea, and *vice versa*.

(2) That the finite understanding can not grasp the infinite;

(3) That the finite understanding can not of itself understand anything except that which is limited by something outside; because as it has not the power to understand everything alike, just so little has it the power, for instance, to undertake or to begin to understand this rather than that, or that instead of this. Since it can do neither of these things, it can comprehend nothing.

The first (or *major*) proposition may be proved as follows:

If man's imagination were the only cause of his ideas, it would be impossible for him to comprehend anything. But he can comprehend something;

Therefore, etc.

The first is proved by the first principle; namely that there is an infinite number of knowable things. According to the second principle, that because the human understanding is limited it can not understand everything, if it were not limited by external things to grasp this thing rather than that or that rather than this, then according to the third principle it would be impossible to understand anything at all.[4]

---

[4] Furthermore it is also false to say that this idea is imagination, for it is impossible to have it different from what it is, and this will now be shown on the following page.

It is indeed true that from one idea which has once come to us from a thing itself and then becomes generalized by us *in abstracto*, we afterwards imagine in

From all this the second can be proved, which
is that the cause of the idea in man is not his imagination but some external cause which compels
him to understand one thing rather than the other;

---

our understanding many particulars to which we then
also may add many others and the abstract attributes
of other things. But it is impossible to be able to do
this without having first known the thing itself from
which they are abstracted. Once determined that this
idea is imaginary, then all other ideas which we have
must be no less imaginary. This being the case, whence
comes such a great difference among them? For we see
some which can not possibly exist, for instance, the mon-
sters which are constructed of two natures, as if a beast
and a bird should exist together, and other similar ones
that cannot possibly have a place in nature which we
know to be differently ordered.

There is a second class of ideas which may possibly
exist but not necessarily, whose essence, however, is
always necessary whether they exist or not. Such are
the idea of a triangle, of love in the soul apart from
the body, etc. Accordingly although I first thought that
I had imagined them, yet afterwards I was compelled
to say that they exist none the less, and would although
neither I nor any man had ever thought of them. And
for this reason then, they are not imagined by me and
must also have a subject (*subjectum*) outside of me
which is not myself, without which they could not be.

Besides these there is still a third idea which is but
one single one, and this involves a necessary existence
and not, as the foregoing class, only the possibility of
existing; for their essence was necessary, but not their
existence, but of this both essence and existence are
necessary and without them it is nothing of itself. Accordingly I now see that no truth, essence or existence of

and this only means that those things whose objective existence he understands, exist formally and are nearer to him than other things. So since man has an idea of God it is clear that God must exist formally, but not concretely since outside of him and

---

anything depends upon me, for as it is shown in the second class of ideas, they are what they are without me, either according only to their essence or according to both their essence and existence. And so indeed much more do I find this to be also true of the third idea, not only that it is not dependent on me, but on the contrary, that it alone must be the subject of what I affirm of it. Thus if it were not, I would be able to affirm nothing at all of it, as is the case with other things although they are not essential; yes, it must even be the subject of all other things. Then besides the fact that it is clearly evident from what has been said that the idea of infinite attributes belonging to the perfect being is not imagination, we shall add the following:

After the preceding investigation of nature we have not found as yet more than two attributes belonging to this all-perfect being. And these do not give us satisfaction with which we can content ourselves, as if they included all of which this perfect being should consist; but on the contrary we find in ourselves a something that openly informs us of not only more attributes but even of more infinite perfect attributes belonging to this perfect being before it can be said to be perfect. Now whence comes this idea of perfection? This something can not be produced by these two, for two can yield but two, and not an infinite number. Whence, then? Never from myself, or I must be able to give that which I had not. From where else, then, except from the infinite attributes themselves, which tell us that they exist without telling us also what they are, for of two we know only what they are.

above him there is nothing more essential or more excellent. That man has an idea of God is clear because he understands God's attributes [5] which attributes, however, he will not be able to produce, because he is imperfect. But since he understands these attributes it is therefore apparent that he knows that the infinite cannot be composed of various finite parts; that there cannot be two infinite beings but One only; that this being is perfect and unchangeable, because we know well that nothing of itself seeks its own destruction; and further that it can not change [6] itself into anything better because it is perfect, as it would not be otherwise; and also that such a being can not be subject to whatever comes from without, for it is omnipotent; etc.

From all this it clearly follows that we can prove God's existence both by *a priori* and *a posteriori* methods. Yes, even better *a priori* for whatever can be proved *a posteriori* must be explained by its

---

[5] "*God's attributes*," better, "because he understands that which belongs to God"; for things are not attributes of God. Of course without these God would not be God, nor is he God by virtue of them because they express nothing substantial, but are only like adjectives which require substantives to make them comprehensible.

[6] The cause of this change would have to be either external or internal. It can not be external for a substance which like this exists of itself, is not dependent on anything outside, and therefore is subject to no change from without. Neither can the cause be internal for nothing, much less this, will destroy itself. All destruction comes from without.

external causes, which is an evident imperfection in that it can not be known of itself, but only by means of its external causes. God, however, the first cause of all things and even the cause of himself, manifests himself through himself. Therefore the saying of Thomas Aquinas, that God can not be proved *a priori*, because, indeed, he has no cause, is of but little importance.

CHAPTER II

WHAT GOD IS

After we have proved as above that there is a God it is now time to demonstrate *what* he is; that is, we would say that he is a being to whom all, or an infinite number of attributes are ascribed,[1] of which attributes each in its way is infinitely perfect.[2] In order to express our meaning clearly we shall make the four following statements:

(1) That there is no such thing as limited substance,[3] but that all substance must be infinitely

---

[1] The reason is that since Nothing can have no attributes, the *All* must have all attributes; and so since nothing has not any attributes because it is nothing, the Something has attributes because it is something. Therefore the greater the something is, the more attributes it must have, and consequently God who is the most perfect, the infinite, the Everything, must have infinite and perfect attributes and every attribute.

[2] In Eth. I, def. vi, God is defined as "Substantiam constantem infinitis attributis, quorum unumquodque æternam et infinitam essentiam exprimit," "a substance consisting of infinite attributes, each one of which expresses eternal and infinite essence."— Tr.

[3] Being able then to show that there can be no limited substance, all substance must be unlimited and belong to the divine essence. This we prove as follows: (1) Either it must have limited itself or another must have limited

perfect after its kind; that is to say, that in the infinite understanding of God no substance can be more perfect than it already is by nature.

(2) That there are no two substances alike.

(3) That one substance can not produce another.

(4) That in the infinite understanding of God

---

it. It has not limited itself for as it is unlimited it would have to change its own nature. Neither is it limited by another, for this must be limited or unlimited; it can not be the former, hence the latter — therefore it must be God. He must have limited it because he lacked either power or will, but the first is contrary to omnipotence, and the second to goodness. (2) That there can be no limited substance is clear from the fact that it would then be necessarily obliged to have something that it has obtained from Nothing, which is impossible. For whence has it that with respect to which it is different from God? Certainly not from God for he has nothing imperfect or limited; therefore then from where else than from nothing? Therefore there is none but unlimited substance. Whence it follows that there can not be two like unlimited substances, for if this is assumed limitation necessarily follows. And from this again it thus follows that one substance can not bring forth another. The cause that should produce this substance must have the same attributes as that which is produced as well as just as much perfection, or more or less. The first is not true for then the two would be alike; nor the second, for one would be limited; nor the third, for from Nothing can no Something be produced. Further if the limited came from the unlimited then would the unlimited be limited. Therefore one substance can not produce another. From this it again follows that all substance must exist formally, for if it does not exist there is no possibility for it to be able to be produced.

there is no substance except that which exists formally in nature.

Concerning the first statement, " that there is no
such thing as limited substance," etc., lest any should
wish to support the opposite view, we would ask
whether then this substance is limited by itself, that
is to say, so that it has willed to make itself thus
limited and not unlimited?   Then whether it is such
by its own cause, which cause has either been not
able or not willing to endow it more?   The former
is not true because it is not possible that a substance
should wish to limit itself, and especially a substance
that was self-caused.   Therefore then I say, it is
limited by its cause which is necessarily God.   Further then if it is limited by its cause, this must be
either because the cause has not been able or has
not desired to endow it more.   That he is not able
would contend against his omnipotence; [4] that he

---

[4] To reply to this that the nature of a thing demands
such and such and therefore can not be otherwise, is
to say nothing, for the nature of a thing can demand
nothing when it does not exist. If you say that we
nevertheless can see what belongs to the nature of a
thing which does not exist, this is true with reference
to existence (*quo ad existentiam*) but not at all with
reference to its essence (*quo ad essentiam*) and here
lies the distinction between creating and generating. To
create is to represent an object according to existence
and essence at the same time (*quo ad essentiam et existentiam simul*); but to generate means that an object
is produced only as concerns its existence (*quo ad existentiam solam*). And therefore there is no creation
in nature but only generation. Accordingly when God

· should not wish to endow it more although fully able savors of ill-will, which in no sense belongs to God who is all goodness and fullness.

The second statement "that there are not two substances alike," we can prove to be true because every substance is perfect after its kind; for if there were two alike then must one necessarily limit the other and consequently not be infinite, as we have shown before.

Then concerning the third statement, to-wit: "that one substance can not produce another," lest someone again might maintain the opposite, we would ask whether the cause which was to produce this substance had the same attributes as the created substance, or not? The latter cannot be true for out of nothing something cannot be produced. Therefore the former hypothesis must be true. And then we ask again whether the attribute which is to be the cause of the created object is just as perfect as this created object, or less or more perfect. Less it can not be we say for the above mentioned reason. Neither can it be more, we say, because then the second must be limited which would contradict what

---

creates, he creates the nature of the object at the same time as the object itself. And he would be unkind if while he had the power he would not have the desire to so create an object that it would correspond to its cause in both essence and existence (*in essentia et existentia*). But that which we have here called "to create" can not properly be said to have occurred, and we would only call attention to what we have to say concerning the distinction between creating and generating.

we have already proved. Therefore then it must
be just as perfect, therefore like it, and two like
substances are clearly contrary to our former demonstration.

Moreover that which is created is by no means
produced from nothing but must necessarily be
created from that which actually exists. But that
something should have been produced from him,
which after it had been produced from him he would
not then have less, that we cannot grasp with
our understanding. Finally if we would seek
the cause of the substance which is the principle of
the things that arise from its attribute, then it remains for us again to seek the cause of the cause,
and then again the cause of that cause, and so on
in infinitum; so that if we are obliged to stop some-
where as we must, it is necessary that we settle upon
this one substance.

The fourth statement, " that in the infinite understanding of God there is no substance or attributes
except such as formally exist in nature," can and will
be proved by us (1) from the infinite power of
God, because in him there can be no cause by which
he can be moved to make one thing in preference
to or better than another; (2) from the singleness
of his will; (3) because he cannot leave any good
thing undone as we shall soon see later on; (4) because it would be impossible that that which does
not yet exist should be able to appear; because one
substance can not bring forth another. And what
is more, if this were true there would be no more

infinite substances than there are, which is absurd. From all these it follows that all is predicated of nature in all, and that nature accordingly consists of infinite attributes each of which is itself perfect in its way, which agrees with the accepted definition of God.

Against what we have just said, namely that there is nothing in the infinite understanding of God except what exists formally in nature, some people will argue in this wise: If God has made everything, then he can make nothing more; but that he should not be able to create anything more contends against his omnipotence. Therefore, etc.

In regard to the first, we grant that God can create nothing more. And as to the second we would say that we admit that if God should not be able to create what can be created it would contend against his omnipotence, but by no means if he could not create that which is self-contradictory; just as if we were to say that he has made everything and yet should be able to make still more. And surely it is a much greater perfection in God that he has created all that existed in his infinite understanding, than that he should not have created, or as they would say, should never have been able to create. But why say so much about it here? Do they not themselves argue thus,[5] and must they not thus argue; If God is omniscient then he can not know

---

[5] That is, whenever we argue from this the admission that God is omniscient, then they can not argue otherwise.

more; but that he can not know more is contradictory to his perfection; therefore, etc? But if God
has everything in his understanding, and by his infinite perfection cannot know more; why then can we
not say that he had also brought forth all that he
had in his understanding, and brought it about that
it either exists formally in nature or will exist?

Because we now know that everything is alike in
the infinite understanding of God, and that there
is no reason why he should have created this in
preference to or better than that; and that he could
have produced everything in the twinkling of an eye,
so let us see whether we cannot adopt the same
weapons against our opponents that they have used
against us in this way: If God can never create
so much but that he should still be able to create
more, then he can never make what he can make;
but that he cannot create that which he can create
is self-contradictory;

Therefore, etc.

The reasons then why we have said that all these
attributes which are in nature comprise but one being
and by no means different beings (for we can understand them clearly and distinctly, the one without the
other) are as follows:

1. Because we have previously found out that
there must be an infinite and perfect being, by which
nothing can be understood except a being of which
all must be predicated in all. And why? Attributes must be ascribed to a being which has any existence, and the more existence is ascribed to him,

the more attributes must be ascribed to him; and consequently if the being is infinite his attributes must also be infinite [6] and just this is what we call a perfect being.

2. Because of the oneness which we see everywhere in nature. For if there were different [7] essences in nature one could not possibly unite with the other.

3. Because just as we have seen that one substance cannot produce another, and also that if a substance does not exist it is impossible that it could begin to be, yet nevertheless we see that in no substance (of which however we know that it exists in nature) considered separately is there any necessity actually to exist, since existence does not belong to its particular essence.[8] Hence it must necessarily

---

[6] Prof. E. E. Powell (*Spinoza and Religion,* p. 109) says that in this passage he translates *oneyndelijk* " infinite in number and extent," and adds, " His [Spinoza's] use of the word in either sense and in both at the same time often accounts for a lack of precision of thought."— Tr.

[7] That is, if there were different substances that were not referred to a single essence union would be impossible, because we see clearly that they have nothing at all in common except thought and extension, of which we, nevertheless, consist.

[8] That is, if no substance can exist otherwise than actually and yet essence does not follow from its existence; if it is grasped in the abstract it follows that it must not be anything particular, but something which is an attribute of something else, that is to say, of the All-one and All-existent. Or thus: All substance exists actually and no essence of any substance taken for itself,

follow that nature which comes from no cause, and
of which we nevertheless know well that it exists,
must necessarily be a perfect being to which existence belongs.

From all this that we have thus far said, it appears that we regard extension as an attribute of
God; which surely can be in no wise true of a perfect
being; for since extension is divisible, the perfect
being must needs be composed of parts, and this
can by no means be said of God because he is a
single being.   Moreover, since extension is divided
it is passive, and this also can not in any sense be
true of God, who can suffer nothing from anything
else, since he is the first efficient cause of all.

To which we answer (1) that part and whole are
not true or actual beings but only thought-entities,[9] and consequently in nature [10] there is neither

---

follows from its nature. Therefore then no actual substance can be grasped by itself but must belong to something else. That is if with our understanding we understand substantial thought and extension, then we understand them in their essence and not in their existence.
But in that we have shown that it is an attribute of God,
we have shown *a priori* that it exists, and *a posteriori*
(with reference only to extension) we prove it from
the modes which must necessarily have it for their subject (*subjectum*).

[9] *Wezens van reeden.*— Tr.

[10] In nature, i. e. in substantial extension; for if it were
divided its nature and essence would be at once destroyed,
since it only consists of infinite extension or in being
whole, which is the same.

But if you should ask, Is there no part in extension

whole nor part. (2) A thing that is composed of various parts must be so constructed that its parts taken separately can be conceived and understood the one with the other. As for instance in a clock which is made up of many different wheels, cords and other things; in this clock, I say, every wheel and cord, can be separately conceived and understood without necessarily comprehending the whole as it is put together. Similarly also water consists of straight oblong particles and each part of it can be conceived and understood without the whole, but extension is a substance which cannot be said to have parts since it can become neither smaller nor larger,

---

for all modes? I say " Not at all." " But," you say, " since there is motion in matter, it must be in part of the matter, but not in the whole because that is infinite for whither could it be moved? There is nothing outside of it. Hence motion can only be in a part." To reply; there is no motion alone, but motion and rest together, and these are and must be in the whole, for there is no such thing as part in extension. If you still say so, tell me then, if you divide the whole of extension, can you also according to nature separate from all parts that part which you cut off with your understanding? And if this is done I ask what is there between the part which is cut off and the rest? You must say either vacancy or another body, or extension itself — there is no fourth alternative. It is not the first for there is no vacuum which is positive and yet not a body; nor the second, for then there would be no mode, but this cannot be, for extension as extension exists exclusive of and before all modes. Hence the third. remains; and so there is no part, but a whole extension.

and no parts of it can be conceived separately because in its nature it must be infinite. And that
this must be true now follows because if extension
were not as it is but should consist of parts, then it
would by no means be infinite as has been said; but
it is not possible that parts could be conceived in an
infinite nature for all parts are intrinsically finite.
Moreover, if it consisted of different parts then it
would be understood that if some of the parts were
destroyed extension itself would remain and would
not be destroyed with the destruction of some of the
parts; a matter which is clearly contradictory with
respect to that which by its own nature is infinite
and can neither ever be, nor be understood to be,
limited or finite. Further as regards division in nature we would say, as has been said before, that
division never takes place in the substance but always and only in the modes of the substance. I,
then, wishing to divide water, divide only the mode
of the substance and not the substance itself, and
this mode now of water and again of something else
remains always the same.

Accordingly division or passivity takes place always in the mode; just as when we say that man
passes away or is brought to naught, it is only understood about man with regard to his being a composite and mode of substance, and not the substance
upon which he himself depends.

As for the other, we have already established, as
we shall also say again, that there is nothing outside of God, and that he is an *immanent cause*.

But when the active and passive are different, passivity is a palpable imperfection, for the passive must necessarily depend upon that outside of itself which has caused the passivity, which cannot occur with God who is perfect.   Furthermore of such an actor who acts of himself, it can never be said that he has the imperfection of passivity because he is not acted upon by anything else; just as there is understanding, which, as the philosophers say, is a cause of its ideas, but inasmuch as it is an immanent cause, how dare we say that it is imperfect as long as it is acted upon by itself?   Finally substance can be called active with greater right than passive because it is the principle of all its modes.   And with these remarks we consider everything satisfactorily answered.

Still the further objection is made that there must necessarily be a first cause which moves this body, for when at rest it is impossible for it to move itself; and since it is clearly evident that there is both rest and motion in nature, it is thought that they must necessarily be produced by an external cause.   But it is easy for us to answer this, for we grant that if the body was a thing self-caused and possessed no attributes except length, breadth and thickness, then there could be within itself no cause to begin to move it if it were at rest; but we have previously shown that Nature is a being of which all attributes may be predicated; and since this is the case nothing can be wanting to produce all that is to be produced.

As we have hitherto spoken of what God is, we

shall now in one word say how those of his attributes which are known to us exist in both thought and extension, for here we speak only of attributes which might be properly called the attributes of God, by which we come to know him in himself and not as operating outside of himself. All that men ascribe to God besides these two attributes, must be (if they otherwise belong to him) an external designation, in the same way that he is self-caused, eternal, one, unchangeable, etc.; or, I would say with respect to his operations, in the same way that he is a cause, a foreordainer, a ruler of all things, which are all characteristic· of God, without, however, giving knowledge of what he is. Yet how and in what manner these attributes are nevertheless to be found in God, we shall show hereafter in the following chapters. But for a better understanding and a closer elucidation of the foregoing we have thought it well to add the following discourse, consisting in a

CONVERSATION

BETWEEN

UNDERSTANDING, LOVE, REASON AND DESIRE

Love (to Understanding). I see, Brother, that my essence and perfection are entirely dependent upon thy perfection; and since the perfection of the object which thou hast comprehended is thy perfection, and again since mine is begotten of thine, now tell me, I beseech thee, whether thou hast comprehended a being that is perfect in the highest degree, not being able to be limited by anything else, and in which I also am comprehended?

Understanding. For my part I do not contemplate nature otherwise than in its entirety, infinite and perfect in the highest degree, and if thou shouldst doubt it, ask Reason who will explain it to thee.

Reason. The truth of this seems to me unquestionable, for if we wished to limit nature, we would have to limit it with a Nothing, which is an absurdity, and at the same time with the following attributes, that it is one, eternal, and of itself infinite; and we will escape this absurdity by stating that it is one eternal unity, infinite, omnipotent, etc., hence that nature is infinite and that everything is comprehended in her; and the negation of this we call " Nothing."

Desire. Well, but this agrees remarkably with the fact that the unity and diversity which I see everywhere in nature, complement each other. And how? I see that *intelligible* substance has nothing in common with *extended* substance, and that the one excludes the other; and if besides these two substances thou assertest still a third which is perfect in all particulars, thou wilt surely entangle thyself in evident contradiction for if the third is placed outside of the two first, it will lack all the attributes which these two possess, which cannot be in a whole outside of which nothing exists. Moreover if this being is omnipotent and perfect, it will be so because it has caused itself, and nothing else; and yet that would be more powerful which having brought forth itself could also bring forth another. And finally if thou wouldst call it omniscient it is necessary that it should know itself, and at the same time thou must understand that the knowledge of oneself alone is less than the knowledge of oneself together with the knowledge of other substances, all of which are evident contradictions. And therefore I would advise Love to be satisfied with these things which I point out to her, and not look for other things.

Love. And what, thou villain, hast thou shown me except that which would directly occasion my downfall? For if I had ever joined myself to that which thou hast pointed out, I would this moment be pursued by two chief foes of the human race, namely hate and remorse, and often also by oblivion. And therefore I turn once more to Reason in order that he may go on and stop the mouth of these foes.

Reason. When thou sayst, O Desire, that thou dost see diverse substance, thou art mistaken I tell thee; for I see clearly that there is but *one only which exists of itself and is possessed of all other attributes.* And if then thou wilt call corporeal and intelligible things " substances " in relation to the modes which are dependent on them, then thou must also call them " modes " in relation to the substance on which they depend; for considered as self-existent they would seem incomprehensible. And in the same manner that will, feeling, understanding, love, etc., are different modes of what thou callest a thinking substance, which thou wouldst bring all together and make into one, then I, too, conclude from thine own demonstration that infinite extension and infinite thinking together with other infinite attributes (or according to thee, other *substances*), are nothing else than modes of the unique, eternal, infinite self-caused being; and of all these we predicate one single thing, or a unity, outside of which nothing can be conceived.

Desire. It seems to me that I see very great confusion in thy manner of speaking, for thou seemst to imply that the whole should be something distinct from or exclusive of its parts, which of course is absurd. For all philosophers agree in saying that the whole is a secondary knowledge,[11] and that there is nothing in nature but human comprehension. Moreover, as I judge from thy illustrations, thou dost confuse the whole with its cause, for as I say, the whole only consists of or exists by its parts, and for this reason thou conceivest of the thinking power as a thing upon which depend understanding, love, etc. And thou couldst not call it a whole, but a cause of the effects thou hast mentioned.

Reason. I certainly see how thou hast summoned all thy friends against me, and so that which thou hast not been able to accomplish by thy false reasoning, thou intendest now to do by the use of ambiguous words, as is the common practice of those who take a stand in opposition to truth — and yet thou

---

[11] Schaarschmidt translates *kundigheid* here by " Axiom."— Tr.

shalt not succeed by these means to win Love to thy
side. Now thou sayst that the cause, in so far as it is the
author of effects, must therefore be outside of them.
And this thou sayst because thou knowest only of the
transeunt and not of the *immanent* cause which latter brings forth nothing at all outside of itself, as
for instance understanding which is the cause of its
ideas. And therefore I called the understanding
a cause in so far as, or seeing that, its ideas depend
on it,[12] and again a whole, with reference to the
fact that it is made up of its ideas; so also God for
his effects or creations is nothing else than an immanent cause and also a whole, considering the
second remark.

SECOND CONVERSATION
BETWEEN
ERASMUS AND THEOPHILUS

(Serving partly to support the foregoing and
partly relating to the Second Part following.)

Erasmus. I have heard thee say, O Theophilus,
that God is the cause of all things, and therefore
that he can be none other than an immanent cause.
If he is an immanent cause of all things how then

---

[12] Schaarschmidt says that there is manifestly an error
here in the Dutch MS. and unnecessarily combines this
and the last clause of the preceding sentence into one:
" So wird z. B. der Verstand, welcher die Ursache seiner
Begriffe ist, deswegen auch von mir, sofern oder hin-
sichtlich dessen, dass seine Begriffe von ihm abhangen,
eine Ursache."— Tr.

canst thou call him the more remote cause? for that would be impossible in an immanent cause.

Theophilus. When I said that God is a more remote cause I said so only with reference to the things which God (without any other formality than just his existence) had brought forth directly; but by no means have I called him absolutely a remote cause, which thou shouldst have plainly inferred by my words, for I said that *in a certain way* we might call him a remote cause.

Erasmus. I understand now entirely what thou didst mean to say; but I also observe that thou hast said that the product of the internal cause is united in such a way to its cause, that together they make a whole. And if this is so, then it seems to me that God cannot be an immanent cause, for if he makes a whole together with what is brought forth by him, then thou ascribest more being to God at one time than at the other. Remove this doubt from me, I pray thee.

Theophilus. If thou wouldst escape from this confusion, Erasmus, give heed to this one thing which I shall now say to thee. The essence of a thing does not increase by combination with another thing with which it makes a whole; but on the contrary the first remains unchangeable. I will give thee an example that thou mayst better understand me. A sculptor has made many wooden figures after the likeness of the parts of a human body; he takes one of these which has the form of a human bust, and puts it together with another that has

the form of a man's head, and of the two he makes
a whole which represents the upper portion of a
human body.   Wouldst thou say then, that the essence of the head had increased because it was
joined to the bust?   That is not true for it is the
same as it was before.

For greater clearness I shall give thee another
instance, namely an idea which I have of a triangle,
and another [idea] produced by extending one of
the angles of the triangle which extended or extending angle is necessarily equal to the two opposite inner angles.   These I say, have brought forth
a new idea, which is that the three angles of the
triangle are equal to two right angles.   And this
notion is so connected with the first, that without
the one the other could not exist or be understood.
And of all the notions which everyone has we make
a whole, or what is the same, a thought-entity,
which we call "understanding."   Thou canst now
see plainly that although this new notion is united
to the previous one, no change occurs in the foregoing, but on the contrary it remains without the
slightest alteration.   And thou canst say the same
of every idea which in itself Love brings forth, for
Love in no way strengthens the nature of the idea.

But why heap up so many examples, since thou
canst clearly see it thyself in the example of which
we were just now speaking?   I have plainly showed
that all attributes which depend on no other cause
and to define which no species is necessary, belong
to the essence of God, and because created things are

not able to provide an attribute, the essence of God is not increased by this means however closely it is united with it. Hence it follows that the whole is only a thought-entity, and is not distinguished from the general except in that the general is made up of different ununited individuals, but the whole is composed of different united individuals; and also in that the general includes only parts of the same kind, but the whole may include parts both of the same and another kind.

Erasmus. As far as this is concerned thou hast satisfied me. But besides this thou saidst that the effect of the internal cause cannot perish as long as its cause endures, which I see is certainly true. But since it is true, how can God then be an internal cause of all things when many things are nevertheless destroyed? According to the former distinction thou wilt say that God is properly a cause of those effects which he has directly brought forth without any other means than his own attributes, and that these then as long as their cause lasts cannot pass away; but that thou dost not call God an internal cause of the effects whose existence does not depend directly upon him, but which have arisen from some other thing, while their causes do not and can not operate without and outside of God, and which can therefore also perish since they are not brought forth by God directly. But this does not satisfy me, for I see that thou dost infer that human understanding is immortal because it is an effect that God has produced in himself. Now then

it is impossible that anything was necessary to bring
forth such an understanding except the attributes
of God; for in order to be a being of such exceeding
perfection it must have been created from eternity
like all other things which depend immediately upon
God, and if I do not deceive myself I have heard thee
say so.   If this is true how wilt thou reconcile this
without leaving a difficulty unsolved?

Theophilus.   It is true, Erasmus, that the things
which for their existence' sake have occasion for
nothing else but the attributes of God, have been
directly created by him from eternity.   But it must
be observed that although it is necessary that for the
essence of a thing a particular mode (*modificatio*)
be required and a thing outside of the attributes of God, that therefore God would not cease
to be able to bring forth a thing directly, for of the
necessary things which were required to produce a
thing, there are some to produce the thing, and
others in order that the thing can be produced.   As
for example: I wish to have a light in a certain
room; I light one and by itself it illuminates the
room; or I open a window, which action will not
of itself make it light, but nevertheless brings it
about that the light can enter the room.   And in this
manner for the motion of one body another body
is required which must possess all the motion which
passes from it to the other.   But in order to create
in us an idea of God, no other particular thing is
required which possesses that which is created in us,
but only a body in nature whose idea is necessary

in order to demonstrate God directly. This too thou hast been able to conclude from my words; for God, as I have said, is known only through himself and not through anything else. But this I tell thee, that so long as we do not have a clear idea of God which unites us to him in such a way that it leaves us not a thing to love besides himself, we can not say truly that we are one with God and depend directly upon him. Now whatever thou mayst still have to ask, leave it until another time; just now my time is required for something else. Farewell.

Erasmus. There is nothing more for the present, but I will now occupy myself with that which thou hast said until another opportunity. May God keep thee!

CHAPTER III

GOD IS THE CAUSE OF EVERYTHING

We shall now begin to discuss the attributes which we have called properly God's (*eigene*),[1] and first of all we shall show how he is the cause of all things. We have already said that one substance can not bring forth another, and that God is a being of whom all attributes are predicated; whence it clearly follows that all other things can neither exist nor be comprehended without or aside from him. Wherefore we may say in all reason that God is the cause of all things.

Considering then that we are accustomed to divide the efficient cause in eight parts, in the same way let us investigate how and in what respect God is a cause.

1. We say that he is an *effluent* or *productive* cause of his works; and, as far as there are results, an *active* or *efficient cause* which we will call the same, as they are interrelated.

2. He is an *immanent* and not a transeunt cause

---

[1] The following were called God's proper attributes because they are like adjectives which cannot be understood without their substantives. That is, without these God would not be God, but yet he is not God by virtue of these, for they yield nothing substantial while God consists only of substance.

32

inasmuch as he operates within and not outside of himself because outside of him there is nothing.

3. God is a *free* and not a natural cause, as we shall point out and make entirely clear when we shall discuss whether God can avoid doing what he does, and then it will be shown in what true freedom consists.

4. God is a cause by virtue of himself and not by accident; which will appear later on in the discussion of predestination.

5. God is a *principal* cause of the works which he has created directly, as there is motion in matter, etc., in which the less principal cause can find no room since it is always in particular things; as when he dries up the sea with a hard wind and so forth in all particular things that there are in nature.

The less *important-originating* cause is not in God because there is nothing outside of him that can confine him. But the *preëminent* cause is his perfection itself, by which he is the cause of himself and consequently of all other things.

6. God alone is the first or *originating* cause, as has been seen by the foregoing demonstration.

7. God is also a *general cause* but only in so far as he produces various effects. Otherwise he can not be said to be for he needs no one in order to produce effects.

8. God is the *proximate* cause of things which are infinite and unchangeable and which we say have been created directly by him, but in one sense he is the *ultimate* cause of all individual things.

CHAPTER IV

GOD'S NECESSARY WORKS

We deny that God is able to leave undone that which he does, and shall prove this also when we shall discuss predestination, where we shall show that all things depend necessarily upon their causes; but secondly this is better proved by the perfection of God, for it is true beyond all doubt that God can perform as perfectly as has been conceived in his thought. Likewise things understood by him can he not understand more perfectly than he understands them; hence all things can be performed by him so perfectly that they can not be made more perfect by him.

In the next place when we conclude that God could not avoid doing what he has done we derive this from his perfectness; because it would be an imperfection in God to be able to leave undone what he does, without, however, attributing to God a less important originating cause which should have influenced him to action, for then he would not be God.

But now the dispute again arises whether he can leave undone all that which is in his thought and which he can perform so perfectly, and whether such an omission is a perfection in him. Now we say that because all that happens is brought about by God, it must therefore necessarily be predestined by him, otherwise he would be changeable, which would be a great imperfection. This must have been predestined by him from eternity, in which eternity there is no before or after, whence it follows surely that God has never been able to predestine things in any other way than as they have now been determined since eternity, and that God could exist neither before nor without these conditions. Further if God should leave something undone this must happen either from a cause in him or from none; if the former, it is necessary for him to leave it undone; if not, he must necessarily be obliged not to leave it undone. This is clear enough. Further, in a created thing it is a perfection to exist, and to be caused by God, for of all imperfections the greatest is non-being. Because the well-being and perfection of all is the will of God, if God should will that this thing were not to be, then the well-being and perfection of that thing should always consist in non-being, and this in itself is contradictory. In consequence of this we deny that God can leave undone that which he does. Some people think this is a slander and belittling of God, but this judgment comes from not rightly grasping wherein true freedom consists. It is by no means, as is thought, to be able to do or to leave undone something good or bad, but true freedom is nothing else but the first cause, which is not at all confined or forced by anything else, and by its perfection alone is the cause of all perfection. Consequently if God could leave it undone, he would not be perfect, for to be able to leave undone the performance of good or perfection in that which he produces, would not be possible for him except by some deficiency.

Then that God alone is the only free cause is now clear not only from what has been said but also from the following, namely that outside of him there is no external cause which could compel or constrain him, which is not the case with created things.

Against this the following arguments are brought: The good is good only because God wills it, and this being the case he can probably bring it to pass that evil would become good. But such an argument is just as valid as if I said, God is God because he wills that he is God, therefore it is in his power not to be God, which is absurdity itself. Further, when men do something and the question is asked why they do it, the answer is " Because right conduct demands it." If then it is asked why righteousness, or better, the first cause of all that is righteous, has so demanded, the answer must be " Because righteousness wills it so." But can righteousness, I wonder, refrain from being righteous? Not at all, for then it could not be righteousness. But those who say that God does all that he does because it is good in itself, these, I say, may possibly think that they do not agree with us. But this is far from true, for they set something before God to which he is to be pledged or bound, namely a cause which requires that this should be good and that again be righteous.

Further the question arises whether God would

be just as perfect even if all things since the beginning had been made by him or arranged and
predetermined differently than they are now. To
this the answer would be that in case nature had
been created from all eternity different from what it
now is, it must necessarily follow according to the
position of those who ascribe will and understanding to God, that then God would have had both
another will and another understanding according
to which he would have acted differently; and so we
are obliged to conclude that God would be differently constituted than now, and if we assume that he is
now most perfect, we would be compelled to say that
he was not so at the time when he created all things
differently. All of which under the circumstances
implies in itself the most palpable absurdity, and can
by no means be applied to God who now, from the
beginning and to all eternity is, was, and ever shall
be unchangeable.

This was further proved by us in the definitions
which we have given of a free cause; which does
not mean that it should be able to do something
or to leave it undone, but only that it does not depend on something else; that is to say, that all that
God does is done and performed by him as by the
freest cause. If then he had made other things in
the past differently from what they are now, it must
surely follow that at some time he has been imperfect, which is false. For considering God as the
first cause of all things, there must be something
within him by which he does what he does, and does

not leave it undone. Because we say that freedom
does not consist in either doing something or not
doing it, and because we have further shown that
that which makes him do something can be nothing
else than his own perfection, so we infer that if it
were not his perfection which caused him to do it,
the things would not be and could not have become
what they now are. This is the same as if we said,
" If God were imperfect then things would now be
different than they are."

So much for the first attribute! Now we shall
pass to the second which we call properly God's
and see what we shall have to say about it, and so
forth to the end.

CHAPTER V

GOD'S PROVIDENCE

The second attribute of God which we call properly his (*proprium*) is *providence* which to us is nothing else than the endeavor which we experience both in nature as a whole and in particular things, tending towards the maintenance and guarding of their own existence. For it is evident that nothing by its own nature should be able to attempt its own destruction, but on the contrary that everything in itself makes an effort to keep itself in its present condition or to bring itself to a better one. So then according to our definition we assume a general and a particular providence. The general is that providence by which every object is brought forth and maintained in so far as it is a part of nature as a whole. The particular providence is the striving of everything in particular towards the preservation of its own essence in so far as it is regarded not as a part of nature but as a whole. And this is explained by the following example: All the members of a man's body are provided and cared for in so far as they are parts of the man, which is general providence, and the particular providence is the effort of every particular limb (as a whole and not as a part of the man) towards the guarding and maintenance of its own welfare.

CHAPTER VI

GOD'S PREDESTINATION

We call divine predestination the third attribute.

(1). We have shown previously that God can not leave undone that which he does; that is to say, that he has created everything so perfect that it can not be more perfect.

(2). And moreover, that nothing can occur or be understood without him.

It remains to consider whether there are any accidents in nature, that is, whether there are some things which can either happen or else not happen, and secondly whether there is anything of which we can not ask why it exists.

But that there are no accidental things we prove thus: It is impossible for anything to exist which has no cause for existence. That which is accidental has no cause. Therefore, etc.

The first is beyond all dispute, and the second we shall prove thus:

If something which is accidental has a certain definite cause for being, it must then be necessary; but that it should be both accidental and necessary at the same time is contradictory. Therefore, etc.

Perhaps some one will say that an accidental thing has no certain definite cause, but an accidental one. If this were so it must be true in either a divided (*in sensu diviso*) or composite (*in sensu composito*) sense; that is to say, either that the essence of the cause (since it is the cause) is not accidental; or that it is accidental that that something (which should be necessary in nature) shall be a cause that the accidental thing should happen. However, both the one and the other are false.

For in regard to the first, if the accidental *something* is accidental because its cause is accidental, then the cause must also be accidental because the cause which caused it is also accidental, and so on *in infinitum*. And now because it has been shown above that everything depends upon one cause only, the cause also would have to be accidental, which is evidently false.

Then in regard to the second; if the cause were not more limited to produce one than the other, that is, to create this something or not, it would be impossible for him to both create it and not create it, which is directly contradictory.

Now with regard to the second point abovementioned, that there is no object in nature of which we can not ask why it exists, this makes it possible for us to say that it rests with us to investigate by what cause something actually exists, for it is impossible for the non-existent to be something.

This cause we must seek either within or outside of the object. But if the question is asked according to rule for the sake of investigation, we say that none at all seems to be necessary; for if existence belongs to the nature of the object it is certain that we must not seek the cause outside of it. But if this is not the case with this something, then must we indeed look outside of it for the cause. But since the first belongs to God alone, it is therefore proved (as we have also done now as previously) namely that God alone is the first cause of everything. And hence we see further that this and that will of man (for the existence of the will does not belong to its essence) must have also an external cause by which it was necessarily caused; that this is so appears from all that we have said in this chapter, and shall appear even more in Part II when we shall mention and discuss human freedom. [Pages 147 ff.]

Against all this, others ask how is it possible that God who has been said to be the supremely perfect, and the only cause, disposer and provider of all things, permits such confusion (notwithstanding his power), everywhere in nature. Then too, why has he not created man so that he could not sin?

In the first place it can not be said with justice that there is confusion in nature, considering that no one knows all the causes of things enough to judge of them. Such an objection arises from the ignorance which postulates general ideas with which it is thought particular ideas must correspond in order to be perfect. These *ideas* are then assumed to be in the understanding of God, just as many of Plato's imitators have said that these general ideas (such as " reasonable," " animal " and the like) are created by God. Although the followers of Aristotle say that these things are not actualities, but thought-entities, nevertheless they often consider them to be material things, since they have clearly said that God's care does not extend over individuals but only over the race; for instance, that God did not regard Bucephalus and other particular horses, but only the race of horses as a whole. They say also that God has no knowledge of particular and transitory things but only of the general which according to their opinion are permanent. But we have been justified in calling this ignorance in them, for in the first place only particular things have a cause and not generalities because they are nothing.

God, then, is a cause and provider only of particular things. Hence particular things will have to conform to another nature, and thus are not able to conform to their own, and consequently are not what they really are. For instance, if God had made all men like Adam before the fall, then he would have only created Adam and neither Peter nor Paul, while it is exactly God's perfection that he gives existence to all things from the smallest to the greatest; or rather, that he has everything complete within himself.

With regard to the other objection as to why God has not made man without sin, it will serve to reply that all which has been said of sin was said only with reference to the comparison of two things with each other, or the same under different aspects. If a clock, for instance, that would not strike and indicate the hours, conformed to the ' purpose of the maker, men would say it was good, and if it did not so conform they would say it was bad, notwithstanding that it might be good in itself, if only the maker's purpose had been for it to strike out of time and wrong.

We shall conclude then by saying that Peter must necessarily conform to the idea of Peter, and not with the idea of a person. Good and evil, or sins, are only modes of thought and by no means things that have [objective] existence as we will perhaps show more extensively in the future, for all operations and things that exist in nature are perfect.

CHAPTER VII

THE ATTRIBUTES WHICH DO NOT BELONG TO GOD

At this point we shall now begin to speak of the attributes[1] which are usually ascribed to God and yet do not rightly belong to him; likewise of those by which men try, though vainly, to demonstrate God, and also of the laws of accurate definition.

In order to do this we shall not trouble ourselves greatly with the images which men have usually formed of God, but we shall only investigate briefly what the philosophers can tell us of him. Now they have described God as a self-existent being,

---

[1] The attributes of which God consists, are nothing but infinite substances each of which must itself be infinitely perfect. That this must necessarily be so, reason convinces us clearly and distinctly, but it is true that of all these infinite attributes only two are as yet known to us by their own being, and these are thought and extension. All things else that are usually ascribed to God are not attributes but only certain modes which might be attributed to him either in consideration of all of his attributes, or in consideration of one attribute. In consideration of *all,* that he is the eternal, self-caused, infinite and unchangeable cause of all things; in consideration of one, that he is omniscient, wise, etc., which pertains to thought, or again that he is omnipresent, fills all [space], etc., which pertains to extension.

the cause of all things, omniscient, omnipotent, eternal, single, infinite, the supreme good, of infinite compassion, and so on, but before we enter upon this investigation let us first see what they grant us.

First they say that no true or lawful definition of God can be given since according to their opinion every definition must consist of species and [specific] differences, and as God is no form of any genus he therefore can not be rightfully and legitimately defined.

In the second place they say that God can not be defined because the definition must depict the object exactly and affirmatively. Therefore, since we can know nothing of God affirmatively, but only negatively according to their hypothesis, no legitimate definition of God can be given.

Moreover they have also said that because God has no cause he can never be proven *a priori* but only plausibly or from his effects. So because they admit sufficiently in their hypothesis that they have but a very slight and trifling knowledge of God, we may proceed to study their own definition.

In the first place we do not see that they give us here any attributes (*attributa*) by which we may know what the object (God) is, but only certain properties (*propria*) which may belong to an object and yet never explain what the object is. For although self-existent, cause of all things, the supreme good, eternal and unchangeable, and so forth, apply only to God, nevertheless we can not know from these qualities what the being is to which these properties belong, and what attributes it has.

It is now time for us to consider these attributes which they ascribe to God and yet which do not belong to him, as omniscient, compassionate, wise and so forth, which can not be attributed to him who is a being existing by nothing but himself, because they are but certain modes of the thinking object, and can by no means exist or be understood without the substances of which they are the modes.

Finally they call him the supreme good; but if by this they understand anything else than what they have already said, to-wit: that God is unchangeable and the cause of all things, they have become confused in their own notion, or do not rightly understand themselves. This results from their error in regard to good and evil, in that they consider man himself to be the cause of all his sin and evil, and not God. But according to what we have already proved, this can not be, or we would be compelled to suppose that man is then also the cause of himself. But this will appear more clearly when we treat later of the will of man. It is now necessary for us to unravel the sophistry with which they try to excuse their ignorance of the knowledge of God.

They say first that a legitimate definition must consist of a species and a [specific] difference. Yet although all logicians admit this, I do not know where they get it, for surely if it were true, we could not know anything. For if we must

first know an object perfectly by means of a definition consisting of species and difference, we can
never know perfectly the highest species which has
no species above it. Now then! If this highest
species which is the cause of our knowledge of all
other things is not known, much less can other
things be known and understood which are explained by means of that species. Yet since we are
free and do not regard ourselves as in the least
bound to their propositions, we shall bring forward
different laws of definition according to true logic,
that is to say, according to our own division in
nature.

We have seen that attributes (or " substances "
as others call them) are things, or to express it
better and more exactly, self-existent entities [2] which
for this reason manifest themselves through themselves. We see that other things are merely modes
of the attributes, without which they also could
not exist, or be understood. Therefore there must
be two kinds of definitions: (1) of the attributes
which belong to a self-existent being, and which
need no species or anything by which they may be
understood or explained, for since they are attributes of a self-existent being, they also would be
known of themselves, and (2) those which do not
exist of themselves but only by virtue of the attri-

[2] Here the grammar of the Dutch sentence is confused.
The subject is in the plural while the predicate and
verb are in the singular: " dat de eigenschappen zaaken,
of . . . een door zig zelfs bestaande wezen is."—Tr.

butes of which they are the modes, and through which as belonging to their species they must be understood.

So much concerning their proposition about definitions. As regards the second, that we cannot have an adequate knowledge of God, this has been sufficiently answered by Descartes in his reply to this objection.

As for the third, that God can not be demonstrated *a priori*, this has already been answered above. Since God is the cause of himself it is enough that we know him through himself and such proof is much stronger than that *a posteriori* which usually occurs only through external causes.

CHAPTER VIII

NATURE AS CREATOR
(*Natura naturans*).

At this point before we go on to something else, we shall briefly divide the whole of nature into nature as creator (*natura naturans*) and nature as creature (*natura naturata*). By the former we understand a being that we clearly and distinctly comprehend by himself and without the aid of anything else than himself, such as the attributes (*attributa*) which we have heretofore assigned to him, and this is God. The Thomists, too, understood God in the same way though their *natura naturans* was a being (as they said) beyond all substances.

We shall divide the *natura naturata* in two divisions, general and particular. The general consists in all the modes which depend immediately upon God, of which we shall treat in the next chapter; the particular consists in all the particular things which are caused by general modes, so that in order to be comprehensible, the *natura naturata* requires substance.

CHAPTER IX

NATURE AS CREATURE
(*Natura naturata*).

We have knowledge of only two general *natura naturata* or modes of creatures which depend immediately upon or are created by God, and these are motion in matter [1] (*stoffe*), and understanding in the thinking thing. We then say that these have been known from all eternity, and will remain changeless to all eternity, truly a work as great as beseemeth the greatness of the Master.

Motion belongs more properly to the treatment of natural science than here, because it has existed from all eternity, and will remain changeless to all eternity, because it is infinite in its kind, and of itself can neither exist nor be understood.— but only by means of extension. All this we shall not discuss here, but shall only state that it is a son, creature or effect directly created by God.

Understanding in the thinking object is likewise a son, product or immediate creation of God, also created by him from all eternity and remaining

---

[1] What is said here of motion within matter is not said seriously for the author expects by this means to find the cause as he has done to some extent *a posteriori*. But this may remain here because nothing is built up or depends upon it.

51

changeless to all eternity. It has but one property, and that is to understand clearly and distinctly at all times, and from this an infinite or absolutely perfect satisfaction invariably arises at not being able to leave undone that which is done. Although what we have said here is clear enough of itself, nevertheless we shall show it more clearly later on in the treatment of the emotions of the soul, and therefore will not discuss it further now.

CHAPTER X

WHAT IS GOOD AND EVIL

Now in order to say briefly what is in itself good or evil we shall proceed as follows:

Some things exist in our understanding and not in nature, and so are only our own work, and serve for the purpose of understanding objects distinctly. Among these we include all relations which have reference to different objects, and we call them *entia rationis*. The question now is whether good and evil belong under the *entia rationis* or *entia realia*, and since they are nothing but relations, it is beyond doubt that they must be placed among the *entia rationis*. For we never say that a thing is good except with reference to something else that is not so good or not so useful to us as something else, and we say that a man is bad only with reference to one who is better, or, in the same way we say that an apple is bad with reference to another that is good or better. All of this could not be called impossible, if it were not better or good in that respect in which it was so called.

' Accordingly when we say that something is good, it is the same as saying it corresponds to the general idea which we have of such things. And therefore as we have heretofore shown, things must

53

correspond to their particular ideas whose essence must be a perfect existence, and not with the general because then they would not exist at all.

The confirmation of what we have just said seems clear to us, yet nevertheless as conclusion to what we have said, we shall add the following proofs:

All things which exist in nature, are either objects or actions. Now good and evil are neither objects nor actions. Therefore good and evil do not exist in nature. For if good and evil are objects or actions they must have definitions. But good and evil (for instance, the goodness of Peter and the wickedness of Judas) have no definition apart from the existence of Peter and Judas; for existence is only in nature and they can not be defined apart from their existence. Therefore as above, it follows that good and evil are neither objects nor actions which exist in nature.

PART II.

MAN AND WHAT PERTAINS TO HIM

.

INTRODUCTION

After having spoken in Part I of God and of universal and infinite things, we now in this second part come to the discussion of particular and limited things. Not all of them, however, for they are countless, but we are to treat only of those which relate to man and among these we shall mention first what man is, in so far as he consists of certain modes comprehended in the two attributes which we have observed in God. I say certain *modes* because I do not at all understand that man is a substance in so far as he consists of spirit,[1]

---

[1] 1. Our soul is either a substance or a mode. But it is not a substance for we have shown that there can be no limited substance in nature; therefore it must be a mode.

2. Since the soul is a mode, it must be a mode either of substantial extension or substantial thought. It is not a mode of substantial extension, for etc.; therefore it is a mode of thought.

3. Since substantial thought can not be limited, it is infinitely perfect in its kind and an attribute of God.

4. A perfect thought must have cognition, idea, mode of thought of each and every actually existing object, whether substance or mode, without exception.

5. We say "actually existing" because we are not speaking of a cognition, idea, etc., which recognizes the whole nature of all essence as being connected in its nature, without their particular essentiality, but only of the

soul and body. For we have already shown in
this Treatise (1) that no substance can have a
beginning, (2) that one substance can not bring
forth another, and finally (3) that no two like substances can exist.

Since man has not existed from all eternity, is
limited, and is like many others, he can not be
a substance; so that all the thoughts that he has are
but modes of the attribute of thought which we

cognition, idea, etc., of particular things which are constantly coming into existence.

6. This cognition, idea, etc., of every particular thing
which comes actually into existence is, we say, the soul
of that particular thing.

7. Each and every particular thing that comes actually
into existence becomes what it is by motion and rest,
and this is the case with all the modes in substantial
existence which we call " bodies."

8. The distinction between them consists only in different proportions of motion and rest, by which this is so
and not otherwise, this is this and not that.

9. From these proportions of motion and rest this
body of ours comes into actual existence; of which then
no less than of other things, a cognition, idea, etc.,
must be in the thinking thing, and hence also our soul.

10. But our body when it was still unborn was in a
different proportion of motion and rest, and consequently
it will be in still another when we are dead, and there
shall be an idea, cognition, etc. of our body in the
thinking thing then as now; but not the same because the
motion and rest will then be differently proportioned.

11. In order then to cause such an idea, cognition, mode
of thought, in substantial thought as this [soul?] of ours,
not just any body is required (for then it would be
known differently than it is) but exactly such a body

have ascribed to God. And again all that he has of form, motion and other things, are likewise modes of the other attribute which is ascribed to God.

And although some people attempt to prove that man is a substance from the fact that the nature of man can not exist or be understood without the attributes which we ourselves admit to be substance, yet this has no other foundation than false representations. For because the nature of the material or body existed before the form of the human body,

---

as contains such a proportion of motion and rest, and no other; for as the body is, so is the soul, idea, cognition, etc.

12. Of such a body then which has and maintains its own proportion, as for instance of 1 to 3, the soul and body will be, as ours are now, subject to constant change but not so great that it passes the boundary of 1 to 3; but the soul will change constantly in the same proportion.

13. And this change in us arising from other bodies which act upon us, can not take place without the soul, which also changes, constantly becoming aware of this change. And the awareness of this change is what we call feeling.

14. But if other bodies affect ours so powerfully that the proportion of motion as 1 is to 3 cannot be kept, the result is death and the annihilation of the soul, in so far as it is only an idea, cognition, etc., of this body containing such a proportion of motion and rest.

15. But, because the soul is a mode in the thinking substance, it can also know and love this as well as extension, and by uniting with substances (which always remain the same) make itself eternal.

this nature can not be peculiar to the human body, for it is clear that in the period before man existed, it could not have belonged to the nature of man.

And if the principle is laid down, that that belongs to the nature of a thing without which it could neither exist nor be understood, we would deny this assertion. For we have already shown that nothing can exist or be understood without God. That is, God must previously exist and be understood before these particular things can exist and be understood. We have also shown that species do not belong to the nature of definition, but that those things which can not exist without others, can also not be understood without them. Since this is the case, what sort of a rule can we lay down by which we may know what belongs to the nature of a thing?

The rule then is this: That belongs to the nature of a thing without which the thing can not exist nor be understood; and yet not this alone, but in such a way that the proposition may always be reversed, so that the predicate also can not exist nor be understood without the thing [as the subject]. Of these modes then of which man consists, we shall now begin to treat in the beginning of the following chapter.

CHAPTER I

OPINION, BELIEF AND KNOWLEDGE

In beginning to speak of the modes of which man consists we shall mention (1) what they are, then (2) their effects, and (3) their cause.

In considering the first let us begin with those which are first known to us, namely certain ideas or the consciousness of the cognition we have of ourselves and of the things outside of ourselves.

These ideas we obtain either (1) merely by belief (which arises either from experience or from hearsay), (2) or we receive them by true belief, or else (3) by means of clear and distinct comprehension.

The first is usually subject to error. The second and third, although they differ from each other, yet they cannot both be wrong. But in order to understand all this more distinctly we will give an example taken from the Rule of Three, as follows: Some one has only heard it said that when in the Rule of Three the second number is multiplied by the third and then divided by the first, a fourth number is found which is in the same proportion to the third as the second to the first. And notwithstanding that those who have stated this proposition to him might have lied, yet he has arranged his operations in accordance with it without having had any more knowledge of the Rule of Three than the blind man has of color, and likewise he has chattered about everything which he may have said on the subject, just as a parrot recites what it has been taught.

Another man of nimbler wit would not be thus convinced by hearsay, but puts a particular calculation to the proof, and when finding it to be in agreement will then believe in it. But it is true, as we said, that this also is subject to error; for how can he be sure that this experiment with one particular example can be the rule for all?

A third man who is not satisfied with hearsay because it might deceive, nor with some particular experience because it cannot be a rule, investigates, with the aid of true reason, which never deceives when rightly employed. This tells him that by virtue of the property of proportion in these numbers the result must be thus and not otherwise.

But a fourth man with the clearest perception of all, has need neither of hearsay, nor experience, nor logical thought, because by his penetration he sees proportion directly in all his calculations.

CHAPTER II

OPINION; BELIEF, AND CLEAR COGNITION

We shall now treat of the different kinds of cognition of which we have spoken in the foregoing chapter; and in passing we will state what opinion, belief and clear cognition are.

We call the first, then, "opinion"[1] because it is subject to error, and never is found in anything of which we are sure, but only in that of which it can be said to be "guessed" or "deemed." We call the second "belief" because the things which we apprehend only by reason we do not see but know only by convincing the understanding that it must be so and not otherwise. But clear cognition we call that which is not convinced by reasoning but by a feeling and enjoyment of the thing itself, and this far surpasses the others.

After this introduction let us now come to their effects, of which we will say that from the first spring all the passions (*passien*) which are opposed to wholesome reasoning; from the second, good desires; and from the third, true and upright love with all its offshoots.

---

[1] The significance which Spinoza attaches to "opinion" seems to be very much the same as the Buddhist idea of "illusion."— Tr.

Then we name cognition as the proximate cause of all the passions in the soul. For we consider it impossible for anyone to be able to be brought to love or desire or any other form of will if he neither understands nor knows the above mentioned reason and modes.

CHAPTER III

THE ORIGIN OF PASSION IN OPINION

At this point let us now see how, as we ·have said, the passions (*passien*) come to arise from opinion. In order to do this thoroughly and intelligibly we shall propose some of them singly and with these for examples prove our statement.

Let us call surprise the first which is found in him who knows things in the first way,[1] [i. e., by opinion]; for, because he draws a general conclusion from certain particulars he stands amazed

---

[1] This does not exactly mean that a formal resolution must precede surprise but that it occurs even without it, just as we though silent believe a thing to be just as we are accustomed to see, hear or understand it to be, and not otherwise. When, for instance, Aristotle says, *Canis est animal latrans,* he therefore concludes that everything that barks is a dog; but when a farmer says "a dog" he means without expressing it the same that Aristotle does with his definition, so that when the farmer hears barking he says, "a dog!" Accordingly if they were to hear another animal bark the farmer who drew no conclusion would be just as astonished as Aristotle who had drawn a conclusion. Further, when we become aware of something of which we had never before thought, it is not that we were not previously acquainted with it in whole or in part, but not as thus arranged in all particulars, or we have never been so affected by it.

whenever he sees something which tends to contradict his conclusion; like the man who has never seen sheep except with short tails, and is surprised when he sees the sheep of Morocco that have long tails. Similarly a story is told of a farmer who had persuaded himself that there were no fields except his own but when upon missing his cow he was compelled to go to search in others far away, he was struck with wonder that besides his own small fields there should be so many other fields. And surely this must be the case with many philosophers who have persuaded themselves that outside of the field or little sphere upon which they live there are no others, because they take none other into consideration. But surprise never draws true conclusions. So much for the first.

The second shall be "love." Since this must spring either from true ideas, or from opinion, or even finally from simple hearsay, we shall first see how it arises from opinion and afterwards from ideas (for the first leads to our destruction and the next to our highest welfare) and then from the last, [i. e., hearsay].

The love that arises from opinion, then, is of such a nature that as often as anyone sees, or fancies he sees, something good, he is constantly inclined to unite himself with it, and for the sake of the good which he observes in it, he chooses it as the best; besides which at that time he knows nothing better nor more pleasant. But when it comes to pass (as usually happens) that he learns

to know something better than this good which
he has known hitherto, he turns his love immediately from the first to the second, which we shall
observe more clearly in the discussion of the freedom of man.

Since this is not the place to speak of love
arising from true ideas we shall pass it by and
speak of the third and last, namely the love which
comes only from hearsay. This we observe generally in children toward their father, in that because the father says this or that is good, they
are drawn to it without being inclined to know
anything further about it. We see this mostly
in those who sacrifice their lives from love of
country, and also in those who fall in love with
something from hearsay.

Hate, the direct opposite of love, arises from
error originating in opinion. For if one person
comes to the conclusion that a thing is good, and
another comes to harm from the performance of
the same thing, then hate arises in him toward the
former which never would occur if men knew
the true good, as we shall presently show. For
all that there is or is thought to be, is nothing more
than wretchedness itself in comparison with the
true good. And is not such a lover of misery more
worthy of pity than hate?

Finally, then, hate can also arise from hearsay
alone, as we have seen in the case of the Turks
against Jews and Christians, of the Jews against
Turks and Christians, of Christians against Jews

and Turks, etc.   For how little do all of these know of the religion and customs of one another!

Desire, whether it consists as some say only of lust or inclination to gain possession of that which one lacks, or, as others prefer,[2] in keeping the things which we already enjoy, it is sure that it can never come to be found in anyone except under the form of good.   Hence it is clear that, like love of which we have just spoken, desire arises from the first kind of knowledge.   For someone who has heard that a thing is good, feels inclination and longing for it, as is seen in the case of a patient who is at once drawn toward such and such a remedy from simply hearing the doctor say that it is good for his ailment.   Desire comes also from experience as is seen in the practice of physicians who are accustomed to look upon a certain remedy as an infallible cure if they have found it to be good in a few instances.

What we have said of these passions can be said of all others, as is clear to everyone.   Then because we are about to investigate which are reasonable for us and which unreasonable, we shall not add more here, but shall close the present discussion of passions which originate in opinion.

---

[2] The first definition is the best, for when the object is enjoyed the desire ceases; the form [of emotion] which we then have to keep the object, is not desire, but fear of losing the beloved object.

CHAPTER IV

WHAT ARISES FROM BELIEF; AND OF THE GOOD AND EVIL IN MAN

Since we have shown in the previous chapter how passions arise from the errors of opinion, let us now see the effects of the two other kinds of cognition, the first of which we have called " true belief." [1]

This then shows us plainly what the thing is said to be but not what it really is, and that is

---

[1] Belief is powerful evidence by reason (by which I am convinced in my understanding) that the thing is actually and to such an extent outside of my understanding, as I in my understanding am convinced. "A powerful evidence by reason," I say, in order by this means to distinguish it both from opinion which is always doubtful and subject to error, and from true cognition which does not consist in a conviction from reason but in a direct union with the thing itself. "That the thing is actually and to such an extent outside of my understanding:" I say "actually" because in this reasoning can not deceive me, for otherwise it could not be distinguished from opinion; "to such an extent," for it can only inform me what the thing is said to be and not what it truly is, otherwise it would not be distinguished from knowledge; "outside" because it makes us enjoy intelligently not that which is within us, but that which is outside.

the reason why it can never bring about our union
with the thing believed. I say then that it teaches us
only what the thing is said to be, and not what it is,
which is a very different thing. For, as we have
said in our example of the Rule of Three, if a man
can find out by proportion a fourth number which
bears the same relation to the third as the second
to the first, so he can say by the use of division
and multiplication that the four numbers must be
in equal ratio; and this being the case he speaks
of it nevertheless as of a thing outside of himself.
But, as we have shown in the fourth example, when
he comes to consider, then he says with truth that
the thing is such in so far as it is within and not
outside of him. So much for the first.

The second effect of true belief is that it brings
us to a clear understanding by which we love God
and this makes us intelligently aware of the things
which are not within us but are outside of us.

The third effect is that it creates in us the
knowledge of good and evil and points out to us
all the passions which are to be destroyed. And
because we have before stated that the passions
which come from opinion are subject to great error
it is worth while to see how the same thing is
shown by this second kind of cognition in order to
see what is good in it, and what is evil.

In order to do this properly, let us observe it
from near at hand in the same manner as before,
in order that we may know which we may choose
and which must be discarded. But before we come

to this let us briefly state what is good and evil in mankind.

We have said before this that all things conform to necessity and that there is no good and no evil in nature, so that what of good or evil we seek in man can be nothing else but a thought-entity (*wezen van reden*). And when we have conceived in our understanding an idea of a perfect man, it should be sufficient cause for us to contemplate ourselves and see whether there is within us also a means by which we may attain to such perfection.

And therefore all that advances towards perfection we shall call " good," and on the other hand that which is a hindrance or prevents progress, " evil."

I must then, I say, comprehend a perfect man if I wish to assert anything about the good and evil in mankind, because treating of the good and evil of Adam for instance, I might confuse a real being (*ens reale*) with a thought-entity (*ens rationis*) which must be strictly avoided by a genuine philosopher, for reasons which we will state in what is to follow or at some other opportunity. Further, because the end of Adam or of any other particular creature is not known to us except by results, so it follows that that also which we can say of the end of man must be founded on the concept of a perfect man in our understanding,[2]

---

[2] For we cannot receive a perfect idea from any particular creature, for this very perfection (whether it is

whose end we well know because it is an *ens
rationis,* and also as has been said, his good and
evil which are but modes of thought.

To come gradually to the point, we have previously shown that the emotions and operations of
the soul arise from the concept of motion and this
same concept we have divided into four kinds, hearsay alone, experience, belief and clear cognition.
And inasmuch as we have seen the effects of all
these, it is therefore apparent that the last one
is the most perfect of all. For opinion brings us
often into error and true belief is good only because it is the way to true cognition, arousing us
to the things which are really lovely. Hence our
ultimate aim and the most excellent that we know
is true cognition. But even this true cognition is
different according to the objects which appear before it, so that the better the object with which
it comes to unite, the better also is this knowledge.
And therefore he is the most perfect man who is
united to God and enjoys him, the most perfect
being.

In order to discover what is good and evil in
passions, let us consider them separately as we have
said. First then — surprise is an imperfection in
the man who is subject to this disturbance because
it arises either from ignorance or prejudice. I say
an imperfection because of itself surprise will not
lead to evil.

---

really perfect or not) can not be deduced except from a
general perfect idea, or *ens rationis.*

CHAPTER V

LOVE

Love, which is nothing else than to enjoy a thing and to be united with it, we shall divide, according to the qualities of the object which man seeks to enjoy and to be united with. Some objects are of themselves transitory; others are not transitory on account of their cause; but a third is everlasting and permanent by its own force and power alone.

The transitory are all the particular things which have not always existed or had a beginning. The second class consists of all the general modes which we have said are the cause of the particular modes; but the third is God, or Truth which is one and the same thing.

Love then arises from the concept and knowledge which we have of a thing, and as the thing is shown to be greater and more splendid our love is accordingly increased within us.

There are two ways by which we may be released from love; either by knowledge of a better object, or by the discovery that the beloved object which formerly was considered great and excellent, carries in its train much mischief and disaster.

But love is of such a nature that we never strive

to be released from it as we might from surprise
and other passions; and there are two reasons for
this, first because it is impossible, and next because
it is necessary that we should not be released from
it.   It is impossible because it does not depend upon
ourselves, but only on the good and benefit which
we observe in the object, and which of course would
not have been known to us if we did not wish
to love it.   But this is not compatible with our
freedom and does not depend upon us, for if we
knew nothing it is very certain that we would not
exist.   It is necessary that we should not be released from love, because on account of the frailty
of our nature we should not be able to exist without having something to enjoy with which we
might be united and strengthened.   Which then
of these three kinds of objects must we choose or
reject?

Because, as we have just said, we must necessarily love something and unite with it in order
to exist on account of the frailty of our nature,
it is certain that we will not be strengthened at
all by loving a transitory object and uniting with
it, inasmuch as it is weak itself and one cripple
can not carry another.   It not only is not helpful
to us but it is even injurious, for we have said
that love is a union with the object that our understanding has judged to be excellent and good, and
by this we understand a union by which love and
the beloved become one and the same thing, or
together make one whole.   Therefore that man will

always be wretched who unites himself to transitory things; for it is impossible that he should be able to escape when they come to suffer. Consequently we conclude that since those are so wretched who love the transitory things which in some sense have existence, how very miserable must they be who love honor, riches and pleasure which have no real existence at all!

Let this be enough to show how reason directs us to part from such transitory things, for the poison and the evil that lurks and is hidden in the love of these things has been clearly proven by what we have just said. But we see this fact incomparably clearer when we observe from what an excellent and glorious good we become separated by the enjoyment of these things.

We have said that transitory things are out of our power, but, lest we be misunderstood, we do not mean to say that we are a free cause dependent on nothing else. When we say that some things are within our power and others outside, we understand by the former those that we perform by order of, or together with, nature of which we are a part, and by the latter, those which being outside of us, are subject to no change through us, inasmuch as they are very far removed from our actual existence so ordered by nature.

Continuing, we shall now come to the second kind of objects which are everlasting and permanent, and yet not so by their own power. Upon a little investigation we will at once become aware

that these are nothing more than modes which depend directly upon God. And because they depend upon God, they are not for us to understand
unless we at the same time have a concept of God,
in whom because he is perfect our love must necessarily repose. In one word, it will be impossible
for us to keep from loving God if we use our
understanding aright.

The reasons for this are clear: First, because
we find that only God alone has being, and all
things else are not beings but modes. Since modes
cannot be correctly understood without the being
upon which they directly depend, and we have
previously proved that if when we love something
we come to know a better object than the one
we love, we invariably fall at once upon the latter
and abandon the first; it follows incontrovertibly
that when we come to know God who has all perfection in himself alone, we must necessarily love
him.

Secondly, when we use our understanding aright
in the cognition of things, we must know them
then in their causes. Now then, since God is a
first cause of all other things, the knowledge of
God according to the nature of things (*ex rerum
natura*) must precede the knowledge of all other
things, because the knowledge of all other things
must follow from the knowledge of the first cause.
True love always springs from the knowledge that
its object is glorious and good. What else then
can follow but that it can be poured out more

ardently upon no one than the Lord, our God, for he alone is glorious, and a perfect good.

So now we see how powerful we count love, and also how it must rest in God alone. What we had further to say about love we shall endeavor to state when we treat of the last kind of knowledge. Here we shall next discuss which of the passions we have to accept and which to reject, as we have said before.

CHAPTER VI

HATE

Hate is the inclination to ward off from ourselves something which has done us some harm. Now it is to be noted that we perform our actions in two ways, with passions and without. With passions, as we ordinarily see in the case of masters toward servants who have committed some offence, and this seldom happens without anger; and without passions, as it is related of Socrates that when he was compelled to punish his servant for the servant's own good, he would not do it, if he found that his anger was aroused against his servant.

Because we see that our actions are performed either with or without passion, we consider it to be clear that the things which hinder or have hindered us without arousing us, can be done away with when necessary; and therefore, which is better, that we shun things with aversion and hate, or that we endure them by virtue of the power of reason without arousing our feelings (for we believe this to be possible)? In the first place it is certain that when we do without passion the things which we are to do, no evil consequence can follow, and since there is no middle term between good and evil we see that as it is wrong to act with passion it must be good to act without it.

But let us consider whether there is any wrong in shunning things with hate and aversion. It is certain that hate which arises from opinion, can find no place in us because we know that what is good for us at one time is bad for us at another, as is always the case with medicines.

Finally it comes to the point whether hate arises in us only through opinion and not also through true reasoning. But in order to find this out, we deem it wise to explain clearly what hate is, and to distinguish it carefully from aversion.

Hate, then I say, is an excitement of the soul against some one who has offended us wilfully and knowingly; but aversion is the excitement against a thing which arises from an infirmity or injury which we either understand or suppose to belong to it by nature. I say " by nature " for if we do not think this to be the case we will not feel aversion for it even though we have received some hindrance or injury, because on the other hand we have some usefulness to expect from it, for when a man is injured by a stone or knife he does not feel aversion toward it on this account.

Having made these remarks let us briefly scan the effects of both hate and aversion. From hate springs sorrow, and if the hate is great it turns to anger which not only, like hate, tries to shun the hated object, but also to destroy it when practicable. From this great hate springs also envy.

But from aversion arises some sorrow because we try to deprive ourselves of something which since it is real must always have its essence and perfection.

From what has been said it can be easily understood that if we use our reason aright we can have no hate nor aversion toward anything, because by so doing we would deprive ourselves of the perfection which inheres in everything. We can also see by reasoning that we can never have any hate at all towards anyone, because we must always change everything in nature for the better, if we wish something of it, either for our own sake or for the thing itself. And because a perfect man is the best thing that we can have present before our eyes, so it is by far the best for ourselves and for each man in particular that we try at all times to cultivate them up to perfection; for not until then can we obtain the most fruit from them, and they from us. The means to this end is to continually observe them so that we may be constantly taught and warned by our good conscience itself for it never leads to our destruction, but always to our well being.

In conclusion we say that hate and aversion have as many inherent imperfections as love on the other hand has perfections, for it always brings about improvement, strength and increase which is perfection, while hate on the contrary makes always for desolation, weakening and destruction, which is imperfection itself.

CHAPTER VII

JOY AND SORROW

Having seen how we may truly say that hate and aversion can never have a place in the minds of those who use their understanding as they should, we shall continue in the same manner and speak of other passions, commencing with desire and joy. Inasmuch as these arise from the same causes from which springs love we can say nothing more about them than that we must remember and bear in mind what we have previously said, and with this remark we will pass them by.

To these we shall add sorrow; of which we may say that it arises only from opinions and opinion arises from it, for it springs only from the loss of a good.

Now we have said above that everything we do must tend toward advancement and improvement, but it is certain that so long as we are sad we make ourselves unfitted to accomplish this, hence it is necessary for us to free ourselves from sorrow which we can do by thinking of means by which we may regain what we have lost if it is in our power. If not in our power it is just as necessary to get rid of it lest we fall into all the misery which sorrow brings in its train. And the same with joy, for it is foolish to wish to restore and improve a lost good by a self-seeking and cultivated evil.

Finally he who uses his understanding aright must necessarily recognize God first of all. Now we have shown that God is the highest good and the entire good; therefore it follows incontrovertibly that he who uses his understanding aright can not fall into sadness. And why? He rests in the good which is the whole good and in which is fullness of all joy and pleasure.

CHAPTER VIII

ESTEEM, CONTEMPT, ETC.

Further we shall speak of esteem and contempt, of high-mindedness and humility, of arrogance and self-condemnation. In order to distinguish carefully between the good and evil in these we will consider them at once.

Esteem and contempt are only in relation to something large or small just as we recognize that certain things are great or small within us or outside of us.

High-mindedness does not extend outside of ourselves and belongs only to him who recognizes his own perfection according to its true value without passion or observing that he is esteemed.

Humility is when a man recognizes his own imperfection without noticing whether he is despised; humility does not extend beyond the humble man.

Arrogance is when a man appropriates unto himself a perfection which is not to be found in him. Self-condemnation (*strafbare Nedrigheid*) is when a man appropriates unto himself an imperfection which does not belong to him. I am not speaking of hypocrites who lower themselves without meaning it in order to deceive others, but of those who think their imperfections are such as they ascribe to themselves.

83

From these observations it is sufficiently evident
of how much good and evil each of these passions
is possessed, for as regards high-mindedness and
humility they proclaim their own excellence.   For
we say that their possessor is truly cognisant of
his own perfections or imperfections which is the
best way (so reason teaches us) to approach our
own perfection.   If we recognize our power and
perfection aright we can clearly see what we should
do in order to attain the end we have in view,
or again if we recognize our faults and powerless-
ness, we can see what we should avoid.

With regard to arrogance and self-condemnation
our definitions show us that they arise out of too
certain an opinion, for we say that they belong
to him who ascribes to himself a perfection which
does not belong to him, and in self-condemnation
directly the opposite is true.

From these remarks we see that arrogance and
blameworthy humility are as evil and destructive as
high-mindedness and true humility are good and
salutary; for the latter not only place their possessor
in a very good position but are at the same time
the right step by which we climb to our highest
welfare; while the former not only hinder us from
attaining our perfection, but will bring us altogether to destruction. Blameworthy humility
hinders us from doing what we otherwise must do
to become perfect, as we see in the case of skeptics
(scepticis) who while denying that man can possess truth, by this very denial rob themselves of

truth. Arrogance causes us to grasp things which lead us straight to destruction, as we see in the case of all those who have thought and still think they can perform miracles together with God, and hence brave fire and water, meeting death most miserably while confidently fearing no danger.

As far as esteem and contempt are concerned there is nothing more to be said except to remind us of that which has previously been said of love.

CHAPTER IX

HOPE, FEAR, ETC.

We shall now undertake to speak of hope and
fear, assurance, despair and vacillation, of courage,
boldness and emulation, of faintheartedness and
fright, and considering them one at a time as is
our custom, we will show which of them are
troublesome and which are helpful — all of which
we can do very easily if we but observe closely the
ideas which we can have of a thing that is in the
future, whether it is good or bad.

The ideas which we have with reference to the
thing itself are, whether we consider that the thing
is possible, i. e., whether it can or cannot happen; or
that it necessarily must happen. This as far as
the thing itself is concerned. Then with reference
to him by whom the thing is conceived; whether
he must do something in order to bring the thing
to pass or prevent it.

From these ideas arise the following emotions:
When we conceive that a future event is good
and ought to happen, the soul receives from this
a form that we call *hope* which is nothing else than
a certain kind of pleasure mixed nevertheless with
some sorrow. And again, when we judge the thing
which may possibly happen to be evil, there comes
from it a form in our soul which we call *fear*.

But when the thing is conceived by us to be good, and that it shall necessarily come to pass, there arises therefrom a security in the soul which we call *assurance*, which is a decided joy not mixed with sadness as is the case with hope. But if we conceive the thing to be evil and that it shall necessarily happen, this is the cause of *despair* in the soul, which is nothing but a sure stroke of sorrow.

Hitherto we have spoken of the passions which are contained in this chapter and have given definitions of them in an affirmative manner expressing an equivalent for each. We can now reverse the process and define them in a negative fashion thus: We *hope* that the evil will not come, we *fear* that the good will not come, we are *assured* that the evil will come, and *despair* that the good will not come.

Having said this much of the passions in so far as they arise from ideas with reference to the thing itself, we have now to speak of those which arise from the ideas relating to those who conceive the thing, to-wit:

When a person must do something in order to produce the thing, and yet comes to no conclusion about it, the soul comes to possess a form which we call *vacillation*. But when a manly determination is made to accomplish a thing which can be performed we call it *courage*, and when the thing is very difficult to accomplish we call it *valor* or *bravery*. But when anyone concludes to do a thing because someone else who did it before him has succeeded well, we call this *emulation*. When someone knows what decision he must make to further a good object and to prevent a bad one, and yet does not do it, this is called *faintheartedness;* and if this is very strong we call it *fright.* Finally *jealousy* is the care that men take to enjoy and retain alone that which they now possess.

Because we now know whence these emotions arise, it will be very easy for us to demonstrate which are good and which evil.

As far then, as hope, fear, assurance, despair and jealousy are concerned, it is certain that they have their origin in evil opinion, for, as we have previously shown, all things have their necessary causes and must necessarily happen just as they do happen. And although assurance and despair seem to have a place in the inviolable order and consequence of causes, this is nevertheless far from the facts if the truth of the matter be known. For assurance and despair never exist unless they have first been hope and fear for in these they have their origin. As for instance, when anyone thinks that that which he still expects is good, he receives in his soul the form which we call hope, and being assured of the supposed good the soul then obtains that restfulness which we call assurance. Now this which we have said of assurance must also be said of despair. But according to that which we have stated in regard to love these can not exist in any perfect human being, for they assume things to which we must not cling because of the changeableness (which has been remarked in the definition of love), to which they are subject; and by which also we must not be repelled as is shown in the definition of hate. And to this clinging and aversion, nevertheless, that man is all the time subject who persists in these passions.

As far as vacillation, faintheartedness and fright are concerned, these proclaim their imperfection by their own kind and nature; for all that they do to our advantage arises only negatively from the result of their nature. For instance, anyone who hopes for something that he thinks will be good, yet is not good, and nevertheless by his vacillation or faintheartedness lacks the courage required to perform it, is freed negatively or by accident from the evil which he thought would be a good. These then can in no wise find a place with the man who is led by true reason.

Finally as far as courage, valor and emulation are concerned nothing more need be said beyond what we have already stated in regard to love and hate.

CHAPTER X

REMORSE AND REPENTANCE

We shall speak now of remorse and repentance, but very briefly. They never occur except from surprise, for *remorse* arises only from doing something which we afterwards doubt whether it was right or wrong, and *repentance* from having done something that is wrong.

Because many people who use their understanding aright, at times go astray, when they lack the requisite habit of using their understanding aright at all times, we might perhaps think that remorse and repentance would bring them nearer to the right, and conclude from this, as the whole world does, that they are good. But when we consider them correctly we shall discover that they not only are not good, but on the contrary that they are harmful, and consequently an evil, for it is evident that we always reach the truth more by reason and love than by remorse and repentance. Harmful are they and evil for they are a certain kind of sorrow which we have previously shown to be harmful, and which we must therefore consider as an evil to be warded off and which accordingly [1] we must also shun and escape.

---

[1] i. e., sorrow. Here Schaarschmidt misinterprets the adverbial *dienvolgende* " accordingly " to be the participle " the following " referring to the " passions " treated in the next chapter.— Tr.

CHAPTER XI

MOCKERY AND JESTING

Mockery and jesting rest upon a false opinion and proclaim an imperfection in the mocker or jester. They rest upon a false opinion in that it is thought that he who is mocked is the first cause of his own actions and that they do not (like other things in nature), depend necessarily upon God. They make known an imperfection in the one who mocks, for either that which is ridiculed is ridiculous or it is not. If not, they make but a poor show in mocking that which does not deserve to be mocked; if it is ridiculous they show therewith that they recognize an imperfection in that which they mock, which they are in duty bound to improve by good reasoning and not by mockery.

Laughter has no reference to another but only to the man who sees something good in himself, and because it is a certain kind of pleasure it is useless to say anything else about it than has already been said of pleasure. I speak of the laughter that is caused by a certain idea which has induced the laugh, and not at all of the laughter that is caused by movements of the spirits,[1] of which it was

---

[1] See Chapter XX.— Tr.

not our purpose to speak since it has no reference to either good or evil.

Of envy, wrath, feeling of injury, we shall say nothing here except that they remind us of what has been said heretofore in regard to hate.

CHAPTER XII

HONOR, SHAME AND SHAMELESS-NESS

We shall now speak briefly of honor, shame and shamelessness. The first is a certain kind of pleasure that every man feels in himself whenever he becomes aware that his actions are regarded and praised by others, without having in view any other advantage or profit. Shame is a certain sadness which takes place within any man when he comes to see that his action is despised by others without having in view any other harm or loss. Shamelessness is nothing else than an absence or throwing aside of shame, not through reason but either from ignorance of shame as with children, wild people, etc., or because men who have known themselves held in great contempt step ruthlessly over everything.

Now that we know these emotions we can also measure the vanity and imperfections which they contain. For honor and shame are not only not profitable according to what we have noted in their definitions, but (inasmuch as they are founded on self-love and on an opinion that man is the first cause of his own actions and consequently deserving of praise and blame) are even harmful and to be rejected.

93

Nevertheless I will not say that men must live among mankind as they would live without them, where honor and shame have no place; but on the contrary I admit that we are not only permitted to employ them when we turn them to the use of mankind and for its improvement, but we may also do the same to the detraction of our own freedom, otherwise perfect and lawful. As for instance; if a man dresses himself expensively in order to be thereby esteemed, he seeks an honor arising from self-love without having any regard for his fellows; but if a man sees his wisdom (by means of which he could be useful to his fellow men) held in contempt and trodden under foot because he wears poor clothing he would do well, for the purpose of helping them, to affect a manner of dressing to which they could not object, thus becoming more like his neighbor in the effort to win him.

As far as shamelessness is concerned, it is so conspicuous that to see its deformities we have need only of its definition and we will let this suffice.

CHAPTER XIII

FAVOR, GRATITUDE AND INGRATI-TUDE

Now will follow favor, gratitude and ingratitude. As far as the first two are concerned they are the inclination of the soul to grant and to do some good thing for one's fellow men. I say to *grant*, when to him who has done good, good is returned again; I say, to *do*, when we ourselves have received some good thing.

I am well aware that almost all people judge these emotions to be good, but notwithstanding this, I dare to say that they can have no place in a perfect man. For a perfect man is impelled by necessity to help his fellow men, and by no other cause, and therefore he finds himself the more in duty bound to help the most godless, according as he sees in him the greater misery and need.

Ingratitude is a contempt of gratitude just as shamelessness is of shame, and that without any regard for reason but only arising out of avarice or an all too great love for one's self, and therefore can have no place in a perfect man.

CHAPTER XIV

GRIEF

Grief shall be the last of which we shall speak in our treatment of the passions, and the one with which we shall close. Grief is a certain kind of sorrow arising from the consideration of a good that we have lost and which there is no hope that we shall ever have again. Its imperfection may be recognized from the fact that we consider it an evil when we but look upon it. For we have shown heretofore that it is evil to bind ourselves and to become attached to things which we may lose easily or at all, and which we can not have as we wish. And because this is a certain kind of sadness we must avoid it, as we have previously remarked with regard to similar things when treating of *sorrow*.

Now I think I have sufficiently demonstrated and proved that it is only true belief or reason which can bring us to the knowledge of good and evil. And so whenever we shall show that the first and most excellent cause of all these emotions is knowledge it is clearly seen that if we use aright our understanding and reason, we shall never be able to fall into any of these which should be rejected or cast aside. I say our " understanding " for I do

96

not think that reason alone is able to free us from all these, as we shall also show hereafter in its place.

But we have here to note as a matter of importance with regard to passions that as far as we see or discover, all the passions that are good are of such a kind and nature that we can not exist without them and that they likewise belong essentially to us, as love, desire and all that pertains to love. But the case is entirely different with those which are evil and must be rejected by us, inasmuch as we not only can live very well without them, but also since we are not just what we ought to be until we have made ourselves free from them.

In order to give still more light upon all this it should be observed that the basis of all good and evil is the love bestowed upon an object, for whenever we do not love that object which alone (*nota bene*) is worthy to be loved, namely God, as we have said before, but the things which in their very kind and nature are transient, thence follow necessarily hate, sorrow, etc., according to changes in the beloved object: hate, when someone takes away the thing loved; sorrow when it is lost; ambition when he leans upon self-love; favor and gratitude when he loves not his neighbor for God's sake.

But in contrast to all this, when man comes to love God who is and always remains unchangeable, it is then impossible for him to fall into this pool of passions. Therefore we propose as a firm and inviolable rule that God is the first and only cause of all our good and an emancipation from all our evil.

It may also be remarked that only love, etc., are unlimited; that is, that the more and more it increases the more excellent it becomes, since it is bestowed upon an object which is infinite. Wherefore it can always increase, which is true of no other thing but this alone. Perhaps this will serve afterwards for us as material from which we may prove the immortality of the soul, and how or in what way it can be true.

CHAPTER XV

THE TRUE AND THE FALSE

Now then, let us consider the true and the false
which demonstrate the fourth and last effect of true
belief. In order to do this we shall first state the
definitions of truth and falsehood. Truth is the
affirmation (or denial) of a thing which corresponds
to the thing itself, and falsehood the affirmation (or
denial) of a thing which does not correspond with
the thing itself. But this being the case it would
appear that there is no difference between the false
and true idea; or, because to affirm or deny this or
that is but a mode of thinking, they have no other
difference except that one corresponds to the fact
and the other not, and in this they do not vary in
fact but only in thought. If this is true it may well
be asked what advantage has the one man with
his truth, and what harm does the other man have
because of his falsehood? and how shall the former
know that his conception or idea corresponds with
the fact more clearly than that of the other?
Finally how does it come about that the one is
mistaken and the other is not?

By way of answer it will first serve to state that
the very clearest things give knowledge of themselves and also of falsehood in such a manner that

it would be great folly to ask how we would be conscious of them, for since we have called them the very clearest things there cannot be any other clearness through which they could be illumined. Hence it follows that the truth reveals both itself and falsehood as well, for truth is made clear by truth, that is to say, by itself, just as falsehood is also made clear by it, but falsehood never reveals or explains itself. So any one who has the truth can not doubt that he has it, but he who remains in falsehood or error may well imagine that he has the truth; just as when a person dreams, he may easily imagine that he is awake, but when one is awake he can never think that he is dreaming.

From the above our former statement is to some extent explained when we said that God is truth, or that the truth is God himself.

Now the reason why one person is more conscious of his truth than another, is because the idea of affirmation (or denial) corresponds entirely with the nature of the thing and therefore has more essence. In order to comprehend this better it may be remarked that understanding (although the word sounds different) is purely passion, that is to say, that our soul becomes so changed that it receives other modes of thought than it had before. If, now, because the whole object has affected him, someone receives similar forms or modes of thought, it is clear that he receives an entirely different impression of the form or quality of the object than another who has not had so many

causes, and so to affirm or deny this, much less
of an effort is required than by becoming aware of
the same object by means of fewer or less important additions. From this we see the perfection
of him who stands upon truth as opposed to the
one who does not. For since one changes easily
and the other with difficulty, it follows that the one
has more permanence and existence than the other;
and so also because the modes of thought which
correspond with the thing have had more causes,
therefore they have more permanence and existence,
and bcause they correspond entirely with the
thing, it is impossible that they can at any time
be differently affected or suffer other changes because we have previously seen that the essence of a
thing is unchangeable — all of which is not the case
with falsehood. With the above all the foregoing
questions are sufficiently answered.

CHAPTER XVI

THE WILL

Since we now know what good and evil, truth and falsehood are, and also wherein the welfare of a perfect man consists, it is now time to come to the investigation of ourselves and see whether we attain this welfare voluntarily or of necessity.

To this end it is necessary to discover what the will is to those who postulate a will, and how it is to be distinguished from desire. We have said that desire is the inclination the soul has towards something it deems good, whence it naturally follows that before our desire directs itself utterly to anything, we first make a decision that that something is good, and this affirmation then (or, generally considered, the power of affirmation, and denial) is called the will.[1]

---

[1] The will taken as affirmation or denial is here distinguished from true belief in that it extends also to that which is not truly good; and for this reason because there is not a clear conviction that it cannot be different, as is and must be the case in true belief because from the latter arise only good desires. But the will may also be distinguished from opinion since it consists of guess and conjecture. Accordingly it can be called a belief in so far as it can also be sure, and opinion in so far as it is subject to error.

The point now is whether this affirmation takes place voluntarily or of necessity; that is, whether we affirm or deny something of a thing without some external cause forcing us to it. But we have shown that a thing which is not explained by itself nor whose existence does not belong to its essence must have an external cause, and that a cause which is to produce something must necessarily produce it. Hence it must also follow that to will [2] this or that particularly, to affirm or deny

---

[2] It is certain that the particular act of will must have an external cause by virtue of which it exists, for since existence does not belong to the nature of its own being it must necessarily exist through the existence of something else.

If we say the efficient cause of itself is not an idea but volition in man, and understanding is a cause without which the will is powerless, that hence the will considered unlimited and understanding as well are not thought-entities but actual beings, then as far as I am concerned when I consider it attentively it seems to me general and I cannot ascribe to it any reality. Even if this is so we must admit that the act of willing is a modification of will, and ideas are a mode of understanding, wherefore then the understanding and the will are necessarily and actually distinct substances for the substance was modified and not the mode itself. If the soul is said to control these two substances then there is a third substance;— altogether such a confused state of things that it is impossible to obtain a clear and distinct idea of it. For since the idea is not in the will but in the understanding no love can arise in the will, according to the rule that a mode of one substance cannot pass over to another substance, for that we should will any-

this or that particularly of anything, must take place through some external cause, just as the definition which we have given of a cause is that it can not be free. Possibly this will not satisfy some who are accustomed to occupy their understanding more with thought-entities

thing of which there is no idea in the willing power involves us in contradiction. You say that on account of its union with understanding the will also perceives that which the understanding comprehends, and therefore then it also loves; but because perception is an idea it is also a mode of understanding, and consequently this can not be in the will even if there was such a union of soul and body. For if we admit that the body is united with the soul according to the common assumption of the philosophers, nevertheless the body will never apprehend, nor will the soul extend in space for in that case, a chimera would be possible in which we would conceive of two substances, but that is false. When people say that the soul governs both the understanding and the will, this is inconceivable, for then they seem to deny the freedom of the will which contradicts it. In order to stop here, since I do not wish to bring forward all that I have in mind against the statement of a created finite substance, I shall show briefly that the freedom of the will does not agree with a continuous creation, that the same work is required of God to keep a thing in existence that is needed to create it, and that otherwise things could not exist a moment; these things being so, nothing can be attributed to it. But it might be said that God has created the will as it is, for since it has not the power to keep itself as it is, much less then is it able of itself to produce anything. If it should now be said that the soul produces by itself the act of willing, I would then ask, by what power? Not by that which has been, for it is no more; nor by that which it

(*entia rationis*) than with the particular things
which actually exist in nature; and in doing so
they look upon this *ens rationis* not as such but
as a reality (*ens reale*).   For inasmuch as man has
now this will and now that he makes in his soul
a general mode which he calls will, just as from
this man and that man he forms an idea of man in
general; and since he does not distinguish sufficiently between actual and thought-entities, it so
happens that he regards thought-entities as things
which exist actually in nature, and so considers that
he himself is the cause of some things, as frequently happens in the treatment of the thing
whereof we speak.   For if the question is asked
why man wills this or that, the answer is because
he has a will.   But since the will, as we have
said, is but an idea of willing this or that, and
therefore only a mode of thought, an *ens rationis*,
and not an *ens reale*, therefore nothing can be
caused by it, for nothing is produced from nothing
(*nam ex nihilo nihil fit.*).   And so it is my opinion,
as we have shown, that the will is not a thing in
nature but only an illusion, wherefore we need not
ask whether it is free or not.

I do not say this in regard to will in general

---

now has, for it really has none by which it would be
able to exist or to endure the slightest moment because
it is constantly being created.   Accordingly since there
is nothing which has any power to maintain itself or to
bring forth anything, there remains only to conclude that
God alone is and must be the efficient cause of all things
and that all acts of will are limited by him.

which we have proved to be a mode of thought, but in regard to willing particularly this or that, which some have counted as affirmation or denial. To everyone then who has given heed to what we have said this will be perfectly clear.   For we have said that the understanding is purely passive; that is, that it is a perception in the soul of the essence and existence of things; accordingly that it is never we ourselves that affirm or deny something of a thing, but it is the thing itself that affirms or denies something of itself within us.

Possibly some will not admit this because it may seem to them that they can affirm or deny something else of a thing than is known to them about it.   But this comes from the fact that they have no comprehension of the concept which the soul has of a thing, without or aside from words.   It is true indeed (as there are reasons to convince us) that by words or other means we give others to understand differently about a thing than we know to be the case; but nevertheless we shall never accomplish so much either by words nor any other means that we ourselves should have a different impression[8] of things than we really have, which is impossible, and clear to all who without the use of words or other symbols rely upon their understanding.

But perhaps some may say in opposition to this:

---

[8] *Anders gevoelen.* Schaarschmidt understands this to be the Dutch translation of the Latin *sentimus,* and translates it by *denken.*— Tr.

If it is not we but only the thing which affirms and denies in us with regard to itself, then only that can be affirmed or denied which corresponds with the thing, and consequently there is no falsehood. For we have said that falsehood is the affirmation or denial of something with regard to a thing which does not correspond to the thing; that is, that the thing of itself does not affirm or deny it. But I am of the opinion that if we would but consider well that which we have said of truth and falsehood we would then see this objection sufficiently answered. For we have said that the object is the cause of that which is affirmed or denied of it whether it be true or false; because when we perceive something with regard to the object, we imagine that the object (although we have but little perception of it) nevertheless affirms or denies this of itself in general; this being most often the case with weak souls who by a slight effect of the object receive a very superficial mode or idea, and besides this they have no other affirmation or denial.

Finally the objection might still be made that there are many things which we both will and do not will, as there is something to affirm of a thing or not to affirm, to speak the truth and not to speak it, and so forth. But this occurs because desire is not sufficiently distinguished from will. For with those who accept the will, will is only that work of the understanding with which we affirm or deny something of a thing without regard

to good or evil. But desire is a form of the soul
by which to obtain or to do something with regard
to the good or evil which is observed in it, so that
according to the affirmation or denial which we
have made of the thing, desire still remains, according as we have found or affirmed a thing to be
good; and this, in their opinion, is the will, while
desire is the inclination which we only have afterwards in order to further it, so that also according
to their own saying, the will may exist without
desire, but desire can not exist without will which
must precede it.

All the activities then of which we have spoken
above, since they are performed by reason under
the aspect of good, or avoided by reason under the
aspect of evil, can be comprehended under the inclination which we call desire and not at all suitably
under the name of the will.

CHAPTER XVII

THE DISTINCTION BETWEEN WILL AND DESIRE

Since it is evident that we have no will to affirm or deny, let us now see the correct and true distinction between will and desire, or what the will really must be which was called by the Latins, *voluntas*.

According to the definition of Aristotle desire seems to be a species which includes two forms. For he says that will is the pleasure or impulse which man has under the aspect of good,[1] whence it seems to me he regards as desire (or *cupiditas*) all inclinations whether for good or evil; but when the inclination is only for the good, or the person who has the inclination has it under the aspect of good,[1] he then calls it *voluntas* or good will; but when it is evil, that is when we see in another the inclination to something that is evil, he calls it *voluptas* or evil will. So that the inclination of the soul does not consist in affirming or denying something, but only an inclination to receive something that appears good, or to flee from what appears to be evil.

So now it remains to ascertain whether this de-

---

[1] *Onder scheyn van goet.* Probably the words *onder scheyn* translate the Latin *sub specie.*— Tr.

sire is free or not, in addition to what we have already said that desire depends upon the concept
of things and that the understanding must have
an external cause, and also besides that which we
have said of the will. Although many people see
plainly that the knowledge which man has of various
things is a means by which his pleasure or impulse
passes from one thing to another, nevertheless they
do not observe what it can be that has come to turn
their pleasure so from the one to the other.

But in order to prove that this inclination is not
according to our own free will, and in order to
represent before our eyes what it is that turns
us from one thing to another we shall imagine a
child who comes to the perception of a certain
thing for the first time. For instance I hold up
to him a little bell which makes a pleasant sound
in his ear thus arousing a desire for the bell. Will
he be able to prevent having this desire or longing?
If you say yes, I would ask how and by what cause?
Not from something which he knows better, I dare
say, for this is all that he knows; and not because
it is bad for him because he knows nothing else,
and this pleasantness is the best that has ever hap-
pened to him. But perhaps he will have the liberty
to put away the desire that he has, whence it would
follow that this desire in us might have a beginning
without our volition but that we should be free to
put it from us. But this freedom can not stand
proof, for what could it be that pleasure would be
able to destroy? Desire itself? Surely not, for

there is nothing that from its own nature seeks its own destruction. What then may it finally be that should be able to turn him from this desire? Nothing else indeed but that he by due order and course of nature should be affected by something that is more agreeable to him than the first. And just as we have said in the discussion of the will that will in man is nothing else than this and that will, accordingly it is nothing else than this and that desire which is caused by this and that concept, since this desire is not something actual in nature but is only conjecturing from this or that particular desire. Since desire is not really something, it cannot actually cause anything. So that when we say that desire is free it is just the same as if we said that this or that desire is the cause of itself; that is to say, that before it existed it had brought to pass that it was to be, which is absurdity itself and cannot be.

CHAPTER XVIII

ON THE PROFITABLENESS OF THE FOREGOING

Since we have seen that man being a part of the whole of nature upon which he depends by which also he is guided, can of himself contribute nothing toward his own welfare and happiness, let us see what profit there is for us in these statements of ours, especially as we do not doubt that to some they will seem not a little offensive.

In the first place it follows that verily we are servants, yea slaves of God, and our greatest perfection lies in the fact that we are such necessarily. For if we relied upon ourselves and were not dependent upon God we should be able to accomplish but very little or nothing at all, and would then have just cause to grieve, especially in contrast to the real state of things, which is that we are so dependent on him, the all-perfect one, that we are also a part of the whole, that is to say, of him, and contribute our part, so to speak, to the accomplishment of so many skilfully arranged and perfect works that are dependent upon him.

In the second place the result of this consciousness is that we will not grow proud after performing a praiseworthy act, for such pride is one reason why we cease to progress when we think we are anything of importance and need nothing further, thus struggling directly against our own perfection which consists in always tending to advance farther and farther; but on the other hand that we will ascribe all that we do to God who is the first and only cause of all we perform and carry out.

Third, besides the true love of our neighbor which this consciousness brings about in us, it so disposes us that we never hate him nor become angry at him, but are induced to help him and bring him to a better condition, all of which is the habit of men who have a great perfection or essentiality.

In the fourth place this consciousness serves also towards the advancement of the common weal, for by virtue of it a judge shall never be able to favor one side rather than the other, and being compelled to punish one and reward the other, he will do it with insight in order to help and improve one as well as the other.

Fifthly, this consciousness frees us from sorrow, from despair, from envy, from terror and other evil passions which, as we shall explain hereafter, are the essence of hell itself.

Sixth and finally, this consciousness brings us to the point where we shall not fear God as others fear the devil whom they have imagined will do them some harm. For how should we be able to fear God who is himself the highest good through which all things that have existence are what they are, as well as we also ourselves who live in him?

This consciousness brings us also to the point where we ascribe everything to God, and love only him because he is the most glorious and most perfect being and so devote ourselves entirely to him for herein consists properly true worship and our everlasting welfare and blessedness.[1]

For the only perfection and the final purpose of a slave and of an instrument is to duly fulfil the duties that are assigned to them. For instance, when a carpenter finds himself best served by his hatchet in the construction of a piece of work, then has his hatchet attained its end and perfection; but if he were to think, " This hatchet has now served me so well that I will let it rest and not require any more service of it," just at that moment the hatchet would be diverted from its purpose and would no longer be a hatchet. The same is true of man. As long as he is a part of nature he must follow nature's laws which means serving God, and as long as he does this it is well for him. But if

---

[1] There is much in this latter portion of the Short Treatise to remind us of expressions of the mystical thinkers before and after Spinoza. This paragraph is an especially pertinent passage and recalls the lines of Johannes Scheffler (translated by Dr. Paul Carus in his short compilation of that mystic's quatrains under the title *Angelus Silesius*):

" The highest worship is
    Like unto God to grow,
  Christlike to be in life,
    In habit, and love's glow." — Tr.

God (so to speak) should will that man should no longer serve him, it would rob man of his happiness and destroy it, because all that he is consists in the fact that he serves God.

CHAPTER XIX

OUR BLESSEDNESS

Having seen the profitableness of this true belief, we shall now attempt to fulfil the promises we have made, and shall investigate whether we, through the knowledge which we have already attained with regard to what is good and what evil, what is truth and what falsehood and what in general is the use of all these — whether we, I say, through this can attain our welfare (in other words the love of God which we have observed to be our supreme blessedness) and also in what way we can become free from the passions which we have judged to be evil.

To speak first of the last mentioned, that is to say, of the release from passions,[1] I say that if we

---

[1] All passions which are contradictory to sound reason (as has been previously shown) arise from opinion. All that is good or evil in them is shown to us through true belief, but neither of these nor both together would be able to deliver us from them. We can then be delivered from them only by the third way and that is by true cognition without which it is impossible that we can ever be delivered, as will be shown later on (page 133 ff.). Is not this the same subject about which others have had so much to say and write under different names? For who does not see how properly we can understand opinion to be sin, belief, the law which re-

suppose that they have no other causes than we have assumed, we shall never fall a prey to them if we use our understanding aright, as we can do very easily [2] since we have a measure of truth and falsehood.

But it remains for us now to prove that they have no other causes, and to do this it seems to me desirable that we study into our entire nature both as regards the body and the spirit, and that we show in the first place that body [3] exists in nature by the form and effects of which we are affected and so become aware of it. And this is because when we come to see the effects of the body and what they cause we shall then find also the first and most important cause of all these desires and at the same time that also through which all these desires can be overcome, whence we can see whether this can be accomplished by reason. And then we shall proceed to speak of our love toward God.

Now to prove that body exists in nature will not be difficult since we all know that God exists and what he is, for we have defined him as a

---

veals the sin, and true cognition, the grace which redeems us from sin?

[2] That is to say, when we have fundamental knowledge of good and evil, truth and falsehood; for then it is impossible for us to be subject to that from which passions arise, for when we know and enjoy the best things the worst have no power over us.

[3] The Dutch has *een lichaam*, but the article is clearly better omitted in English.— Tr.

being of infinite attributes of which each is in
itself infinite and perfect. And since extension is
an attribute which we have shown to be infinite
in its kind, it must necessarily be an attribute of
this infinite being. And because we have also
shown that the infinite being is essential, then it
follows at once that this attribute is also essential.

Moreover, since we have also proved that there
is and can be no being outside of nature, which
is infinite, so it is clearly evident that this effect
of the body, by which we become aware of it, can
come from nothing else but from extension itself
and not at all from something different which has
extension *eminenter* as some would have it, for
this it is not, as we have already seen in the first
chapter.

It remains to observe that all the effects which
we see depend necessarily upon extension, such as
motion and rest, must be attributed to this property.
For in so far as this efficient power was not in
nature, it would be impossible for it to be able
to exist even though it might have many other
attributes, for if something is to produce anything
there must be in that something some essence by
which it more than anything else can produce that
something.

Now what we have said of extension we wish
also to have said of thought and whatever else
there is.

It may further be remarked that nothing exists
within us of which we do not possess the possibility

of being conscious; accordingly when we experience
nothing else within us except the effects of the
thinking thing and of extension we then may say
with assurance that nothing else exists in us.

In order to understand clearly the effects of these
two we shall first consider each by itself alone,
and then the two combined, together with the effects
of one and of the other.

So whenever we regard extension alone we are
aware of nothing else within it but motion and rest,
from which we can then find all the effects which
arise from it. And these two [4] modes of the body
are of such a kind that there can be nothing that
can change them but they themselves. Just as, for
instance, when a stone is standing still it is impossible for it to be moved by the power of thought
or anything else but by motion, whenever another
stone makes it move by virtue of greater motion
than its own degree of rest, just as a moving stone
can not come to rest except through something else
which moves less. Therefore it follows that no
mode of thinking within the body shall be able to
bring about either motion or rest.

In agreement, however, with what we observe
in ourselves, it may easily happen that a body whose
motion tends in one direction, nevertheless turns
toward the other, just as if I were to stretch out
my arm and cause the spirits [5] which heretofore

---

[4] Two modes, because rest is no nonentity (*geen Niet*).

[5] Schaarschmidt inserts *Lebens* in parenthesis, "(*Le-
bens-*)*Geister*," i. e., life-spirits. It is obvious here that

did not have their motion in this direction hence-
forth to take it thither, not always, but according
to the form of the spirits, as will be shown hereafter. The reason is, and there can not be any
other, that because the soul is an idea of the body,
they [body and soul] are so united together that
the soul and body thus combined together make one
whole.

The most important effect of the other attribute
(thought) is such a comprehension of things that
after it [the soul] conceives them, either love, hate
or some other passion will arise. Since this effect
does not involve extension, it [the effect] can not
be ascribed to that extension but only to thought,
so that the cause of all the changes which occur
in this mode [the mode of thought] must by no
means be sought in extension but only in the thinking thing.[6] We can see this in the case of love
whose destruction or awakening must be caused
by the concept which we have said occurs either
because it understands some evil to be in the object
or becomes acquainted with something better. So
whenever these attributes act upon each other, passions arise from the one and the other, by limiting
motions which we have the power to direct whither-

Spinoza means by this concrete figure the spiritual aspect
of existence which in other places he calls " thought " or
" consciousness."— Tr.

  [6] This is the first formulation of the Law of Parallelism
which plays such a prominent part in the psychology of
to-day.— Tr.

soever we will. The operation by which one is
acted upon by the other is as follows: The soul
within the body, as has been said, can indeed bring
it about that the spirits which otherwise would move
in one direction now move to the other, and because
these spirits can be set in motion by the body and
thereby be determined, so it may often happen that
they are set in motion in one direction by the body
and yet by the agency of the soul in another direction, whereby they bring about and cause such
anxieties in us as we are sometimes conscious of
without knowing the reasons for them. For otherwise we usually know the reasons well enough.

Further, too, the soul can be hindered in the
power which it has to set spirits in motion, either
because the movements of the spirits are greatly
impeded or because they are greatly increased, impeded whenever after running rapidly we cause the
spirits to give the body by that same running more
motion than usual, and when we stop we cause it
to become necessarily so much weakened. This
might also happen through the use of too little
food. The spirits are increased by drinking too
much wine or other strong drink, and by becoming
hilarious or intoxicated we deprive the soul of its
power to control the body.

So much for the influence which the soul has
on the body. Let us now consider the influence
which the body has on the soul. As most important we would regard the fact that it makes
itself, and by so doing other bodies as well, per-

ceptible to the soul. And this is caused by nothing else than by motion and rest combined, for the body has no other way than this by which it is able to perform work. So that all that happens to the soul besides these cognitions can not be caused by the body. And because the first that the soul comes to know is the body, the result is that the soul now loves it and becomes united with it. But since we have heretofore shown that the cause of love, hate and sorrow must not be sought in the body, but only in the soul (for all the effects of the body must be produced from motion and rest), and because we see clearly and distinctly that one love is destroyed by the idea that we receive of something else that is better, it evidently follows that if we ever have a consciousness of God, at least as clear as that by which we are conscious of our own bodies, we must then become united to him more closely than with our body, and must be released from the body. I say "more closely," for we have previously seen that without him we can neither exist nor be conceived of, and this is because we know and must know him not through something else, as is the case with all other things, but only through himself as we have said before. Yes, even better than ourselves do we know him, because without him we could not have knowledge of ourselves.

From what we have said heretofore it is easy to conclude which are the principal causes of passion. For as regards the body together with its effects of motion and rest, these cannot affect the soul otherwise than to make themselves known to it as objects, and the soul will be affected by them according to the demonstrations which they hold forth to it of either good or evil;[7] and that not inasmuch as it is a body (for then the body would be the principal cause of passion) but only in so far as it is an object like all other things which would also produce the same effects if thus presented to the soul. (But I will not say here that love, hate and sorrow which originate from conceptions of incorporeal things should produce the same effects as those which spring from corporeal things, for these, as shall be shown hereafter, shall

---

[7] But how does it come to us that we know one to be good and the other evil? *Ans.* Since the objects make us conscious of themselves, we will be affected by each differently. Those then by which we are moved most moderately (according to the proportion of motion and rest in which they consist) are the pleasantest, and the farther and farther they depart from this, the more and more unpleasant. From this arise all kinds of feeling of which we are conscious within us, and which are called impulses (*impulsus*) since they frequently originate through the effects of corporeal objects on our bodies; as, for instance, a man in affliction may be made to laugh and be merry by tickling, wine drinking, etc., of which the soul is conscious, but which it did not bring about. For if the soul brought it about, the merriment would be of a very different kind. For then it is not the body which operates, but the intelligent soul using the body as an instrument, and consequently the more the soul performs, the more perfect is the feeling.

have still other effects according to the nature of
the thing from which the conceptions of love, hate
and sorrow, etc., are awakened in the soul by the
consideration of incorporeal things.)   So that (to
return to our previous discussion) if something else
came to be represented to the soul as more splendid
than the body, it is certain that the body would
then be able to have no power to cause such effects
as it now does.   Whence it follows not only that
the body is not the principal cause of passion, but
also, that even if there were in us something else
besides what we have observed is caused in our
opinion by passions, such, if it were true, could
neither be more active nor operate differently in
the soul than the body now does.   For it could
never be other than such an object as would be
entirely different from the soul and consequently
must show itself in this way and not differently just
as we have spoken of the body.   So that we may
truthfully conclude that love, hate, sorrow and other
passions are caused differently in the soul according
to the form of our several perceptions of things,
and as a result if it [the soul] can ever come to
know the most glorious Being it would be impossible that any of these passions would be able to
cause the slightest disturbance within it.

CHAPTER XX

CONFIRMATION OF WHAT HAS GONE BEFORE

Against what we have said in the foregoing chapter the following objections may be raised:

In the first place if motion is not the cause of passion how can it be that sorrow may nevertheless be driven away by some means as is often accomplished by wine? To which it may be answered that a distinction must be made between the awareness of the soul when it first perceives the body and the judgment which it makes at the same time as to whether it is good or bad.[1]

The soul being thus constituted as has been said, we have shown heretofore that it has the power to move the spirits whithersoever it will, but that nevertheless this power can be likewise withdrawn when by other causes arising from the body as a whole, its form thus regulated is removed or changed, and so in its consciousness arises sorrow according to the change that the spirits cause. This unhappiness is caused by its love for and union with the body.[2]

---

[1] That is, between understanding taken in a general sense, and understanding with reference to the goodness or badness of the thing.

[2] Unhappiness in man is caused by a notion of some

That this is so can be easily derived from the fact that this unhappiness can be helped in one of two ways: either by restoring the spirits to their first form that the soul may be relieved from its suffering, or to be convinced by good reasoning to pay no attention to the body. The first is temporary and may be repeated, but the second is eternal, constant and unchangeable.

The second objection might be this: If we see that although the soul has nothing in common with the body it can nevertheless cause the spirits which should move it in one direction to move it in the other, why then could it not cause a body entirely at rest to begin to set itself in motion? [3]

---

evil which is about to befall him, or of the loss of some good. If it is thus understood, such a notion then causes the spirits to crowd about the heart, and by help of other parts to oppress and close in on it exactly the opposite to what happens in the case of pleasure. The soul is further conscious of this oppression and is full of pain. Now what is it that medicine or wine accomplishes? This, that by its effect it drives away the spirits [compare translator's note on p. 119] from the heart and gives it room again, and the soul becoming aware of this is refreshed in that the notion of evil is diverted by the different proportion of motion and rest provided by the wine and is directed upon something else in which the understanding finds more satisfaction. But this can be no direct effect of wine on the soul, but only of wine on the spirits.

[3] Here then, there is no difficulty in how this one mode works upon the other from which it is infinitely different, for it is a part of the whole because the soul is

Further, why then can they not also move all other bodies, which are already in motion, whithersoever they will?

If we now remember what we have said before of the thinking thing, this will easily remove the difficulty. We said that although nature has various attributes there is only a single being of whom all these attributes are affirmed. Moreover we have said also that there is but one single thinking thing in nature which is expressed in infinite ideas accord-

---

never known without the body nor the body without the soul. This we can trace in this way: [This was evidently intended as a reference list, but the pages are wanting in the MSS.— Tr.]

1. There is a perfect being.........................
2. There can not be two substances..................
3. No substance can have a beginning...............
4. Each in its kind is infinite......................
5. There must be an attribute of thought.............
6. There is nothing in nature of which there is not an idea in the thinking thing arising from both its being and essence...
7. Now consequently, etc.
8. If by the signification of things their essence is understood without their existence, then the idea of essence can not be regarded as something apart by itself, for this can not happen until being coexists with essence; and indeed because there is then an object which did not exist before; for instance, if the whole wall is white there is no this or that about it, etc.
9. This idea then alone, apart from all other ideas can be nothing more than just an idea of such a thing, and not that it has an idea of such a thing, whence it follows that such an idea so considered because it is only a part, cannot have the clearest and most distinct idea

ing to the infinite things which exist in nature.
For if the body receives such a mode as, for instance, the body of Peter and again another as
the body of Paul, it then follows that in the thinking thing there are two different ideas, an idea of
the body of Peter which determines the soul of
Peter, and another of Paul which determines the
soul of Paul.   So then the thinking thing can move
the body of Peter by the idea of the body of Peter,
but not by the idea of the body of Paul; in the
same way the soul of Paul can move his own body
but by no means the body of another, as Peter's.[4]

---

of itself and its objects; only the thinking thing which
is the whole of nature can do this, for a part out of
connection with its whole can not, etc.

10. There must necessarily be a union between the
idea and the object because the one can not exist without
the other, for there is no thing the idea of which is not
in the thinking thing, and there can be no idea but there
must also be the thing.   Further the object can not be
changed without the idea being also changed and *vice
versa,* so that no third alternative is necessary which
would cause the union of soul and body.   But it must
be observed that we are speaking here of such ideas that
arise necessarily from the existence of things together
with the essence in God; but not of the ideas which
effect in us the things now actually shown to us, which
is a very different matter; for the ideas in God do not
arise as with us from one or more senses, which therefore also are almost always affected imperfectly by them,
but from existence and essence according to all that they
are.   Nevertheless my idea is not yours although they
produce one and the same effect in us both.

[4] It is clear that no attribute is to be found in man

And therefore it can not also move a stone which is at rest or lying still, for the stone again makes another idea in the soul. And therefore it is none the less clear that it is impossible for a body which is entirely at rest to be able to be set in motion by any manner of thinking, from reasons given above.

The third objection may be this: We seem clearly to be able to see that we nevertheless can cause a certain state of rest in the body, for after we have moved our spirits [5] a long time we experience the fact that we are tired, which is simply a state of rest which we have brought about in the spirit. But we answer that although it is true that the soul is a cause of this rest, it is so only indirectly, for it does not accomplish the rest from motion directly but only by means of other bodies which it has moved and which must then neces-

---

since he began that did not first exist in nature; and since he consists of such a body an idea of which must necessarily exist in the thinking thing, and the idea must necessarily be united with the body, we fearlessly state that his soul is nothing else than this idea of his body in the thinking thing. And because this body possesses motion and rest (which are proportionate and usually subject to change by means of external objects) and because no alteration in the object can take place without taking place also immediately in the idea itself, it follows that men feel (*idea reflexiva*). But I say it is because there is a proportion of motion and rest, because no effect can happen in the body without these two concurring.

[5] See the second sentence in translator's note, p. 119.— Tr.

sarily have lost as much rest as they have shared
with the spirits. So then it appears from every
side that there is only one and the same kind of
motion in nature.

CHAPTER XXI

REASON

It remains for us now to investigate whence it comes that sometimes although we see that a thing is good or bad, yet we find we are powerless to do the good or avoid the evil; nevertheless sometimes we can. We can easily comprehend this when we consider the causes which we have given of opinion, which we said were the causes of all emotions. We said then that they come either by hearsay or by experience. Because all that we find in ourselves has more power over us than what reaches us from outside, it follows that reason can be the cause of the destruction [1] of the opinions which we have

---

[1] And it makes no difference whether we use the word "opinion" or "passion" here; and thus it is clear why we can not overcome by reason those [passions] which from experience are within us, for these are nothing else in us than an enjoyment of or direct union with something which we judge to be good, and although reason shows us what is better, it does not make us enjoy it. Now that which we enjoy within ourselves can not be overcome by that which we do not enjoy and which is outside of us as is the case with what reason offers us. But if this is overcome it must be by means of something that is more powerful and of this kind will be the enjoyment of or the immediate union with that some-

only from hearsay (and because reason does not reach us from outside), but not at all of those which we have from experience. For the power [2] which the thing itself gives us is always greater than what we receive as the conclusion from a second thing. In this same way we have noticed this difference when speaking of reasoning and of clear understanding (p. 61), taking our illustrations from the Rule of Three. For the power which comes from the understanding of the proportion itself is greater than that from the rule of proportion. And it is for this reason that we have often said that one love is brought to naught by another that is greater, because we would not here include the desires which spring from reason.

---

thing which is better recognized and enjoyed than the former. This being the case the overcoming is always necessary, or else may occur also through the enjoyment of an evil that is recognized as greater than the good enjoyed and follows directly upon it. But experience teaches us that this evil does not always necessarily follow, for, etc. See pages 74 and 116.

[2] We follow Schaarschmidt who translates *mogelijkheid* by *Vermögen* instead of "possibility," as indeed the context suggests that the term is meant to translate the Latin *potentia.*— Tr.

CHAPTER XXII

TRUE COGNITION, REGENERATION, ETC.

Since reason has no power to bring us to a state of well being it remains for us to investigate whether we can attain to it by the fourth and last kind of cognition. We have said that this kind of cognition is not a consequence of something else but comes by means of a direct manifestation to the understanding of the object itself. And if the object is excellent and good the soul is necessarily united with it as we have said of our body. Whence it follows incontestably that it is this kind of cognition which causes love, so that when we come to know God in this way we must necessarily become one with him, for he can manifest himself and be known to us only as the most excellent and best. In this alone, as we have said before, consists our supreme happiness.

I do not say that we must know him as he is, but in order to be united to him it suffices for us to know him only to some extent. For even the knowledge that we have of the body is not such that we know it as it is, or perfectly, and yet what a union! what a love!

That this fourth cognition (which is the knowl-

edge of God) is not a result of something else
but is direct, is evident from the fact which we
have shown before that he is the cause of all
knowledge which can be known only through himself and not through any other thing; but from
this fact also, that we are so united with him by
nature that without him we can neither exist nor
be understood. Therefore because there is such
a close union between us and God, it appears that
we can not understand him otherwise than directly.

We shall now attempt to explain our union with
him through nature and love.

We have heretofore remarked that nothing can
exist in nature which does not have an idea of
itself in its own soul;[1] and that according as the
thing is more or less perfect, the union of the idea
with the thing or with God himself is more or
less perfect. For since all nature is but one substance whose essence is infinite, so all things are
united through nature and made one with God.
Now because the body is the first thing of which
our soul becomes aware, and because, as has been
said, the idea which the thinking subject has of
each thing that exists in nature is the soul of that

---

[1] And here what we have said in the first part at once
becomes clear, that the infinite understanding which we
called the Son of God must have existed in nature from
all eternity; for since God has existed from eternity,
so must also the idea of him have existed in the thinking
thing, that is, in himself, which idea objectively corresponds to himself. See p. 49.

thing, the thing must then necessarily be the first cause of the idea.

Yet because this idea can find no rest in the cognition of the body without passing to the cognition of that without which neither the body nor the idea itself can exist or be understood, it becomes immediately united by love with the latter according to previous cognition. This union is better understood and inferred, as it must be, by its effect on the body, in which we see how by the cognition and desire of corporeal things there come to arise in us, all the effects of which we are continually aware in our body because of the movements of spirits; and also the effects arising from this union shall and must be incomparably greater and more splendid (if our knowledge and love perish for that without which we can neither exist nor be understood and which is by no means corporeal) for these must necessarily be constituted according to the thing with which they are united. And whenever we become aware of these effects then can we say with truth that we are born again. For our first birth was accomplished when we became united with the body by virtue of which such effects and movements of spirits have arisen, but this other or second birth of ours shall take place whenever we become conscious of quite different effects of love corresponding to the knowledge of this incorporeal object; and this second birth is as different from the first as corporeal is from incorporeal, or spirit is from flesh. And this may

the more justly and with greater truth be called
regeneration because from this love and union results for the first time an eternal and unchangeable
permanence as we shall prove.

CHAPTER XXIII

THE IMMORTALITY OF THE SOUL

When we attentively consider what the soul is and whence arises its change and duration, we can easily see whether it is mortal or immortal.

We have said that the soul is an idea in the thinking thing arising from the existence of a thing present in nature. From this it follows that according as the duration and change of the thing, so also must be the duration and change of the soul. In this connection we have observed that the soul can be united either with the body of which it is the idea, or with God, without which it can neither exist nor be understood. Whence it can be easily seen (1) that if it is united with the body alone and the body perishes so also must the soul, for if it loses the body which is the basis of its love, it also must come to naught. But (2) if it is united with something else which is and remains immortal, it on the other hand must also remain immortal. For by what means would it become possible for it to be destroyed? Not by means of itself, for now that it exists it is no more able to change or destroy itself than it was able of itself to begin to exist when it did not yet exist. Accordingly that only which is the cause of its existence must be also the cause of its non-existence when it comes to perish, because it changes or destroys itself.

CHAPTER XXIV

GOD'S LOVE TOWARDS MAN

Hitherto we have considered it sufficient to have shown what is our love to God and what its effects, namely, our perpetual duration. So now we do not deem it necessary to say anything about other things such as joy in God, or peace of mind, since we can easily see what might be said about them from what has already been said. It still remains for us to see (since we have hitherto spoken of our love to God) whether there is also a love of God for us, that is to say whether God also loves men whenever they love him.

But in the first place we have said that to God can be ascribed no modes of thought except those that exist in created things; that accordingly it cannot be said that God loves men, much less that he should love them because they love him, or hate them because they hate him; for we would have to assume that people do such things voluntarily and are not dependent on a first cause, which we have previously shown to be false. Moreover this could cause in God a great changeableness in that he should now begin to love or hate those whom he had not loved or hated before, and would be

139

compelled to this by something outside of himself; but this is absurd indeed.

But when we say that God does not love men this must not be understood as if he, so to speak, merely let them alone, but because man, together with all else that is, so exists in God, and God so consists of all things that there can be no room for any particular love from him towards anything else, since everything consists in one thing only, which is God himself.

From this it further follows that God lays down no laws for men that he may reward them when they fulfil his laws; or, to speak more clearly, that God's laws are not of such a nature that they can be transgressed. For if we would call laws those rules of God which are set forth in nature in accordance with which all things are produced and endure, they are laws that can never be transgressed; as, for instance that the weakest must yield to the strongest, that no cause can bring forth more than it contains within itself, and other similar ones which are of such a kind that they never change and never begin, while everything is arranged and ordered according to them. In brief, all laws which can not be transgressed are divine laws, for the reason that all that happens is not contrary to but in consequence of God's own decree. All laws which can be transgressed are human laws; and the reason is because it does not follow that everything that men decree for their welfare is for the welfare of the whole order of nature, but on the contrary may well be conducive to the destruction of many other things.

Since nature's laws are the more powerful, man's laws are brought to naught. Divine laws are the final purpose for which they exist and are not subordinate, but this is not the case with human laws. For notwithstanding that men make laws for their own welfare and have no other end in view than by means of these laws to further their own welfare, so can this end of theirs (since it is subordinate to other ends which one higher than they has in view in that he lets them operate as parts of nature) also serve to coincide with the everlasting laws of God established from eternity, and in this way to accomplish all results. For instance, although the bees, with all their labor and regular system to which they strictly adhere, have no other end in view than to make secure provision against the winter, yet the man who is in charge of them has a very different purpose in supporting and keeping guard over them, namely, to procure their honey for himself. As far as man also is an individual being, he has no aim beyond where his limited existence can reach, but in so far as he is also a part and instrument of nature as a whole, this end of man cannot be the ultimate end of nature because nature is infinite and must use him also among the rest as one of her instruments.

Having said this much about the law of God, it remains for us to observe that man is conscious of two kinds of law within himself,— the man, I mean, who uses his understanding aright and attains to the knowledge of God. This is accomplished both by the connection which he has with God, and by the connection which he has with the modes of nature, of which one is necessary and the other is not. For with regard to the law which arises from connection with God, man has and must always have before his eyes the laws according to which he must live before and with God, because he never can avoid being always necessarily united with him. But with regard to the law which arises from his connection with the modes this is not so necessary since he can separate himself from men.

Because we assume such a connection between God and men, it may justly be asked how God can make himself known to men, and whether this occurs or could occur by means of spoken words, or directly without using any other medium by which it could be done.

We answer, certainly not by means of words, for man would have to know the meaning of the words before they were spoken to him. As, for instance, if God should have said to the Israelites, "I am Jehovah, your God," they must have known beforehand without the words that there was a God before they could be assured that this was he. For they knew well enough that the voice, thunder and lightning, was not God, although the voice said that it was.

And what we have said in regard to words we

would also say of all external symbols. Hence we deem it impossible that God should be able to manifest himself by means of any external symbol, and we consider it unnecessary that this should happen through any other means than God's existence and man's understanding. For since that within us which must know God is the understanding, and since it is so directly united with him that it can neither exist nor be understood without him, it appears without contradiction that nothing can be so closely joined to the understanding as God himself. It is also impossible to be able to understand God by any other means (1) because such a thing would have to be better known to us than God himself which plainly contradicts all that we have heretofore clearly proved, which is, that God is a cause of our knowledge and of all existence, and that all particular things not only cannot exist without him but cannot themselves be understood; (2) because we can never attain to the knowledge of God by anything else whose being is necessarily limited, even though we may be better acquainted with it, for how is it possible for us to be able to draw conclusions as to an infinite and unlimited thing from one that is limited? For if we observed some effects or a work in nature whose cause was not known to us, it would nevertheless be impossible for us to conclude therefrom that there must be an infinite and unlimited thing in nature in order to bring this forth as a product.

For how can we know whether a number of causes together were required to produce this, or whether there was only one?   Who shall tell us that?

So finally we conclude that in order to manifest himself to men's needs it behooves God to use neither words nor miracles nor any other created thing, but only himself.

CHAPTER XXV

DEVILS

We shall now treat briefly as to whether devils exist or not, in this wise: If a devil is a thing that is opposed to God and has nothing of God, it corresponds exactly with the "nothing" of which we have previously spoken.

If, as some do, we assume him to be a thinking being, that neither wills nor accomplishes good, but puts himself in opposition to God, he is surely very wretched, and if prayers can avail they should be offered for his conversion.

But let us see whether such a miserable being could exist for a moment, and we will find out at once that it could not; for from the perfection of the thing arises all its endurance, and the more existence and divinity it has in itself the more permanent it is. Since a devil has not the slightest perfection, how should he be able to exist? To which we add that constancy or duration in the mode of the thinking thing arises only through the union that such a mode has with God which springs from love. Since exactly the opposite of this union has been stated of devils they cannot exist.

Since there is no necessity to assume the exist-

ence of devils why assume it? For it is not necessary for us (as for some others) to assume devils
in order to find the cause of hate, envy, anger and
similar passions, because we have found them satisfactorily without such fancies.

CHAPTER XXVI

TRUE LIBERTY

In the demonstration of the foregoing we have not only wished to make it clear that there are no devils, but also that the causes which prevent us from attaining perfection (or to express it better, those things we call sins) are in ourselves. We have also shown in the foregoing by reasoning and also by the fourth kind of cognition, how and in what way we may attain our supreme happiness and how passion is to be destroyed — not as is commonly said, that it must first be subdued before we can attain to the cognition and consequently to the love of God, for that would be as if it were desired that someone who was ignorant must first forsake his ignorance before he can arrive at knowledge; but that knowledge only is the cause of its destruction is, as we have already said, clearly evident. Likewise we may conclude from the preceding that without virtue, or rather without the control of the understanding, everything leads to destruction, and we are not able to enjoy any rest but live as if out of our element. And therefore although the power of knowledge and divine love cannot yield an eternal rest for our understanding as we have shown, but only a temporal rest, yet it is our duty to strive after even this inasmuch as those who enjoy it would not wish to exchange it for anything else in the world.

This being the case we can rightfully consider it very absurd when many, even those who in other respects are considered great theologians (*god geleerde*), say that if eternal life does not follow from the love of God, then man should seek the best for himself — as if he would be able to find something that was better than God! This is as foolish as if a fish that cannot live out of water should say, " Since living in the water will not give me eternal life, I will leave the water for the land." Yea, what else canst thou say who knowest not God?

Thus we see that in order to attain to the truth of those things which we have established as pertaining to our happiness and peace, we need no other principle than to consider our own advantage, a thing which it is very natural to do under all circumstances. And since we see that we do not find our happiness but on the contrary our ruin, in seeking after things of the senses, luxuries and worldly pleasures, we therefore prefer to be governed by our understanding. But because this can make no progress unless we have first attained to the knowledge and love of God, it has therefore been proved most needful to seek God. Since from the foregoing remarks and considerations we have discovered that he is the best good of all good,

we were compelled to stand still and rest, for we
have seen that aside from him there is nothing that
can give us any happiness, and that it is true
liberty to be bound with the lovely fetters of his
love and so to remain.

Finally we also see that reasoning is not the
most excellent thing in us, but only like a staircase
by means of which we can climb up to the coveted
place, or like a good spirit who brings us a message
of the supreme good without falsehood or deceit,
in order thereby to arouse us to seek it and to unite
ourselves with it, and it is this union which is
our supreme happiness and blessedness.

So now in order to conclude this work, it remains
to show briefly what human freedom is and in what
it consists. In order to do this I shall consider
the following propositions as securely proved.

(1). The more a thing has being the more active
it is, and the less passive; for it is certain that the
active acts by virtue of that which it possesses,
and that the passive suffers by virtue of that which
it has not.

(2). All passivity which is from non-being to being and from being to non-being must be produced
by an external and not by an internal actor, for nothing considered by itself has in itself cause to be
able to destroy itself when it exists, or to create
itself when it does not exist.

(3). All that is not produced from external causes
can likewise have no connection with them, and

consequently can be neither altered nor transformed by them.   From the two last I conclude this fourth proposition:

(4). No product of an immanent or internal cause (which in my opinion are the same) can possibly perish or be changed so long as its cause remains the same, for a product that is not produced by external causes can not be changed, according to the third proposition; and since nothing can altogether perish except by external causes it is not possible that a product would be able to perish as long as its cause endured, according to the second proposition.

(5). The freest cause and the one that is most worthy of God, is the immanent, for upon this cause the product so depends that without it, it could neither exist nor be understood; nor is it subordinate to another cause.   Moreover they are so united that together they make one whole.

Let us now see what conclusions may be drawn from the foregoing propositions.

(1). Since God's being is infinite it has an infinite activity and an infinite negation of passivity, according to the first proposition.   Consequently the more things are united with God by their greater existence, the more activity they also have and the less passivity, and the more also are they free from change and ruin.

(2). True understanding can never perish for in itself it can have no cause to bring about its destruction, according to the second proposition;

and because it has not been created by external causes but by God, it can not be altered by them, according to the third proposition. And since God created it directly and he alone is an internal cause, it follows necessarily that it can not pass away as long as its cause remains, according to the fourth proposition. Now its cause is everlasting, hence it must also be.

(3). All the products of the understanding which are united with it are altogether the most excellent and must be cherished above all else, for because they are internal products they are altogether the most excellent, according to the fifth proposition, and moreover they are necessarily everlasting for so also is their cause.

(4). All the products which we operate outside of ourselves are the more perfect as it becomes more possible for them to be united to us in order to become of the same nature as ourselves, for in this way they are nearest to internal products; as, for instance, if I teach my neighbor to love luxury, honor, covetousness, it is clear that whether I love them or not, however it is or is not, I am struck and knocked down. Not so, however, if my only aim which I endeavor to attain, is to taste union with God, to produce in myself true thought-pictures and to make these things known to my fellow men. In the same way we can all be partakers of this happiness, since it produces the same desire in them as in me, bringing it about that their will and mine are the same, thus composing one and the same nature which always corresponds in all particulars.

From all that has been said it can easily be comprehended what human freedom [1] is, I therefore define it to be a firm existence which our understanding acquires by means of a direct union with God in order to be able to bring forth ideas within itself and fruits outside of itself corresponding with its own nature, yet without its fruits being subject to any external causes by which it might be either altered or transformed. So it is clear from what has been said, which the things are that are in our power and are subject to no external causes, as we here also and in another way than before have shown the everlasting and constant duration of our understanding; and then finally what fruits we have to cherish above all others.

So now it remains for me to close by saying to the friends to whom I am writing: Be not amazed at these new things, for well do you know that a fact ceases not to be true because it is not accepted as such by many people.[2] And because you are not ignorant of the character of the age in which we live, I will beg you most earnestly to undertake to impart these things to others. I will not say that you should remember all of it at once, but

---

[1] The slavery of a thing consists in being subject to external causes, while freedom on the other hand consists in not being subject to them but freed from them.

[2] This is Spinoza's answer to the prevalent philosophy of to-day three centuries before pragmatism as such was formulated.— Tr.

only that if you ever undertake to communicate it to anyone that no other aim shall impel you except the happiness of your fellow men, being confidently assured that you will not be cheated of the reward of your labors. Finally, if by the perusal of this book difficulties might arise against those things which I have established, I beseech you not to hasten to refute them at once before you shall have pondered over them with sufficient time and consideration. If you do this I feel assured that you will arrive at the enjoyment of the fruits which you have promised yourselves from this tree.

APPENDIX

AXIOMS

1. Owing to its nature substance takes precedence over all its modes (*modificationes*).

2. Things which differ from each other are different either actually or accidentally.

3. Things which are different actually, either have different attributes like thought and extension, or are assigned to different attributes as intelligence and motion, of which the one belongs to thought and the other to extension.

4. Things which have different attributes, as well as those which belong to different attributes, have nothing in common with one another.

5. That which has in it nothing of another thing can not be the cause of the existence of that other thing.

6. It is impossible that that which is a cause of itself should have limited itself.

7. That by virtue of which things persist is by nature prior in such things.

PROPOSITION I

To no substance actually existing can the same attribute be ascribed which is ascribed to another substance; or, which is the same thing, in nature there can not exist two substances unless they are actually distinct one from the other.

Demonstration.

If there are two substances they are different;
and therefore (Axiom 2) they are distinguished
either actually or accidentally; not accidentally, for
then the modes according to their nature would have
existed before the substance, which is contrary to
Axiom 1; hence, actually.   Therefore (Axiom 4)
that cannot be said of the one which was said of
the other.—Q. E. D.

PROPOSITION II

One substance can not be the cause of the existence of another substance.

Demonstration.

Such a cause can contain nothing of such an
effect (Prop. I), for the difference between them
is actual and consequently it [the cause] can not
bring forth that existence.   (Ax. 5.)

PROPOSITION III

All attributes (or substance) are by their nature
infinite and supremely perfect in their kind.

Demonstration.

No substance is caused by another.   (Prop. II);
consequently if it is real it is either an attribute
of God, or, without God, it has been a cause of
itself. If the first, it is necessarily infinite and
supremely perfect in its kind as are all of God's

attributes.   If the second, it is also necessarily the same, for it would not be able to have limited itself.   (Ax. 6.)

PROPOSITION IV

To every essence of substance existence naturally so belongs, that it is impossible to assume in any infinite understanding the idea of the essence of a substance which does not actually exist in nature.

Demonstration.

The true essence of an object is something which is actually distinguished from the idea of the same object; and this something is (Ax. 3) either actually existent, or comprehended in another thing which is actually existent, from which other thing this essence can not be distinguished actually but only modally (*modaliter*); such are the essences of all things that we see which, not actually existing before, were comprehended in extension, motion and rest, and if they are actually existent are not distinguished from extension actually but only modally.   Then, too, it is inconsistent to say that an essence of the substance should be comprehended in this way in another thing, since it would not be actually distinguished from it (Prop. I), and also that it should be able to be brought forth by the subject which includes it (Prop. II), and finally that by its nature it could not be infinite and supremely perfect in its kind (Prop. III).   Therefore because

its essence is not included in any other thing it is
a thing which is self-existent.

Corollary.

Nature is known through itself and not by means
of any other thing.   It consists of infinite attributes
every one of which is infinite and perfect in its
kind, to whose essence existence belongs; so that
there is no essence or being aside from nature which
corresponds closely with the essence of the only
glorious and blessed God.

THE HUMAN SOUL

Since man is a created finite thing, etc., it is needful that what he has of thought, which we call soul, should be a modification of the attribute which we call thought without anything else belonging to its essence except this modification; and as this modification is destroyed the soul also perishes although the attribute itself remains unchangeable. Likewise what man has of extension, which we call body, is nothing but a modification of the other attribute which we call extension; if this also is destroyed the human body no longer exists although the attribute of extension remains unchangeable.

Now in order to understand of what sort this modification is which we call soul, and how it has its origin in the body, and also how its change depends on the body alone (which in my opinion is the union of soul and body) it must be observed:

(1). That the most direct modification of the attribute which we call thought contains objectively the formal essence of all things, and that indeed if we assumed a formal thing whose essence did not exist objectively in the above-mentioned attribute, it would not be at all infinite nor supremely perfect of its kind, which has been contradicted in Prop. III. Since nature (or God) is a being of

which infinite attributes are asserted and which
contains in itself all essences of created things, it
is needful that from everything in thought one
infinite idea should be brought forth which contains
objectively in itself the whole of nature as it really
exists in itself.

(2). It must be observed that all the other modifications, such as love, desire and joy, have their origin in this first immediate modification, so that in
case this did not precede there could be no love, desire nor joy. Whence the conclusion is clear that
the natural inclination which everything has to retain
its body, can have no other origin than the idea of
the objective essence of such a body which is in
the thinking attribute. Further, since to the real
existence of an idea (or objective essence) no other
thing is required except the thinking attribute and
the object or formal essence, it is certain as we
have said that the idea or objective essence is the
most direct modification of the attribute.[1] Consequently in the thinking attribute there can be no
other modification which belongs to the essence of
the soul of anything, than only the idea of such
an actually existent thing which must necessarily
be in the thinking attribute for such an idea bears
in its train the other modifications, love, desire, etc.
Now then since the idea arises from the existence
of the object, the idea is altered or destroyed accord-

---

[1] I call the most direct modification of the attribute that
modification which in order to be real needs no other
modification in the same attribute.

ing as the object is altered or destroyed, and this being the case it is the former that is united with the object.

Finally if we should wish to continue and should ascribe to the essence of the soul that by means of which it can really exist, we would be able to find nothing but the attribute and the object of which we have just now spoken; and neither of these can belong to the essence of the soul, since the object has nothing of thought and is distinguished actually from the soul. As far as the attribute is concerned we have shown that it can not belong to the above-mentioned essence, and this is seen more clearly from what was afterwards said, for an attribute as attribute is not united with the object because it is neither altered nor destroyed although the object may be altered and destroyed.

Therefore then the essence of soul consists in being an idea or objective essence in the thinking attribute arising from the essence of an object which indeed actually exists in nature. I say " of an object which actually exists in nature " without further detail, in order to include not only the modifications of extension, but also the modifications of all the infinite attributes which have a soul as well as extension. And in order to understand these definitions somewhat more particularly, we must pay close attention to what I have just said when speaking of the attributes which I have said are not distinguished according to their existence; for they themselves are the subjects of their being; likewise that the essence of every modification is

contained in the attributes we have just mentioned
of one infinite Being.   Therefore in the ninth chapter of Part I, I have called this idea " a creature
created directly by God," since without anything
being added or taken away, it contains objectively
the formal essence of all things.   And this is necessarily the only thing under consideration, that all
the essences of attributes and the essences of the
modifications comprehended in these attributes are
the essence of one only infinite being.   But it must
be remarked that none of these modifications under
consideration exists actually yet they are equally
contained in their attributes, and because there is
no inequality at all, either in the attribute or in
the essences of the modifications, there can be no
particularity in the idea since there is none in
nature.   But when any of these modes affect their
particular existence and by this means distinguish
in any way from their attributes (because their
particular existence which they have in the attribute
is the subject of their being) one particular then
appears in the essences of the modifications, and
therefore in the objective essences, which are necessarily included by them in the idea.   And this is
the reason why we have used these words in the
definition that the idea arises from an object which
actually exists in nature.   And with this we consider that we have explained clearly enough what
the soul is in general, understanding by this not
only the ideas which arise from corporeal modifica-

tions, but also those which arise from the existence of every modification of the other attributes.

But since we do not have such knowledge of the other attributes as we have of extension, let us see whether we can discover a particular definition with regard to the modifications of extension which is better adapted to express the essence of our souls, for this is our proper purpose.

We shall then suppose it already proven that in extension there is no modification except motion and rest, and that every particular corporeal thing is only a certain proportion of motion and rest, so that if there was nothing in extension except motion alone or rest alone, not a single thing could be shown or could exist in all extension; accordingly that the human body is nothing but a certain proportion of motion and rest. The objective essence of this real proportion which is in the thinking attribute is, we say, the soul of the body, so that when one of these two modifications changes to more or to less (motion or rest) the idea too is changed in the same degree. Thus, for instance, when rest is increased and motion is decreased, that pain or misery is caused which we call cold; if on the other hand this occurs in motion that pain is caused which we call heat. And if it is true (and hence arise the different kinds of pain that we feel when we are struck with a stick in the eyes or on the hands) that the degrees of motion and rest are not the same in all parts of our body but that some have more of motion and rest than others, herein lies the difference in feelings. And if it be true (and hence arises the difference in the feeling of a stroke with wood or iron on the same hand) that the external causes which also bring about these changes vary from one another and do not all have the same effect, there follow differences of feelings in one and the same part. And again, if the change which takes place in one part is a cause of the return to its first proportion, this gives rise to the pleasure which we call rest, delightful exercise and joyousness.

Finally then, since we have now explained what feeling is, we can easily see how there results a reflexive idea or self-knowledge, experience and reasoning.

And from this also (just as because our soul is united with God and is one part of the infinite idea, arising directly from God) the origin of clear knowledge and the immortality of the soul can be clearly seen. But for the present what has already been said will suffice.

GLOSSARY OF TERMS

GLOSSARY OF TERMS

This Glossary makes no pretentions to completeness but may serve for a reference list to some of Spinoza's modes of expression as interpreted by his countryman. The German words are those used by Schaarschmidt in his translation, and are not necessarily limited to the philological equivalents of either Dutch or English.

ENGLISH	DUTCH	GERMAN
absolutely	absoluyt	schlechthin
abstract	afgetrokken afgescheid	abstrahirt abstrakt
absurdity	ongerijmtheed	Ungereimtheit
accidents	gebeurlijke dingen	zufällige Dinge
actual	daadelijk wezentlijk	tatsächlich wirklich
affirmation	bevestiging	Bejahung
after its kind *in suo genere* (I def. VI, Ex.)	in zijn geslagte	in seiner Art
anger	toorn toornigheid	Zorn
angry	vertorent	zornig
anxieties	benaauwtheden	Beklemmungen
apply	toepassen toeschrijven	aufpassen beilegen zuertheilen
apprehend	vatten	fassen
arrogance	verwaantheid	Hochmuth
ascribe assign	toepassen toeschrijven	beilegen zuertheilen
assume	veronderstellen	voraussetzen
assurance	versekerdheid	Zuversicht
attribute *attributum* I, Def. 4	eigenschap	Attribut
aversion	afkerigheyd afkeer	Abneigung

169

ENGLISH	DUTCH	GERMAN
awareness	gewaarworden	gewahr werden
being *ens* (Eth. I Def. VI)	wezen	Wesen
belief	geloof	Glauben
belonging	eigen	eigen
benefit	nut	Nützlichen
blame	laster	Tadel
blessedness	gelukzaligheid	Glückseligkeit
body	lichaam	Körper
boldness	stoutheid	Kühnheit
bravery	dapperheid	Tapferkeit
cause *causa* (I, def. 1)	oorzaak	Ursache
chance	toeval	Zufall
changeable	veranderlijk	veränderlich
choose	verkiezen	erwählen
cognition	kennisse kennen	Erkenntniss
cognizable	doet gewaar worden	wahrnehmbar
complement	te zamen overeen komen	übereinkommen
composite	zamenstel	zusammengesetzt
comprehend	begrijpen	begreifen
comprehension	bevatting	Erkenntnis
conceived	bevat verbeeldt geconcipiert	gefasst vorgestellt
concept	concept idea	Begriff Vorstellung
concretely	uytstekentlijk	auf eminente Weise
conform	overeenkomen	übereinstimmen
confusion	verwarringe	Verwirrung
consciousness	medegeweten gewaar wordende	Bewusstsein gewahr werden
constant	bestandig	beständig

ENGLISH	DUTCH	GERMAN
constituted	gesteld	beschaffen
contempt	versmading	Verachtung
contradiction	tegenstrijdigheit	Widerspruch
control	bestuuren	regieren
convince	overtuigen	überzeugen
corporeal	lighaamelijk	körperlich
correspond	overeenkomen	übereinstimmen .
courage	moed	Muth
creature	schepzel	Geschöpf
custom	zede	Sitte
deem	meynen	dafür halten
definition	beschrijving	Definition
denial	ontkenning	Verneinung
depend on	afhangen van	abhangen von
desire	begeerlijkheid lust	Begierde Lust
despair	wanhoop	Verzweiflung
destroy	vernietigen	vernichten
different	verscheyde	verschieden
directly	onmiddelijk	unmittelbar
disaster	ramp	Schaden
discovery	ondervinding	Erfahrung
disposer	beschikker	Anordner
distinction	onderscheid	Unterschied
diversity	verscheidentheid	Verschiedenheit
divide	deilen	dividiren
divine	goddelijk	göttlich
divisible	deelbar	teilbar
division	deeling schiftinge	Theilung Eintheilung
doubt	twijffelen	zweifeln
effect	uytwerkzel uytwerking	Wirkung
efficient	werkend	werkend

ENGLISH	DUTCH	GERMAN
effluent	uitvloejend	ausfliessend
emotion	tocht	Affekt
emulation	volghyver	Nacheiferung
endeavor	poging	Strebung
enviousness	nijdigheit	Neid
envy	nijt	Neid
error	dooling	Irrtum
essence *essentia*	wezen wezentlijkheid wezentheid	Wesen Wesenheit
esteem	achting	Hochachtung
eternal	eeuwig	ewig
evidence	betuiging	Bezeugung
exclusive of	zonder	ohne
exist	bestaan zijn	bestehen sein
existince *existentia* *existere* I, 7.	wesentheid zijn	Dasein Sein
expect	verwagten	erwarten
experience	ondervinding bevinding	Erfahrung See also *s. v.* dis- covery
extension	uytgebreydheyd	Ausdehnung
external	uytwendig van buyten uytterlijk	äusser
faintheartedness	flaauwmoedigheit	Furchtsamkeit
false	valsche	falsch
falsehood	valsheid	Falschheit
favor	gunste	Gunst
fear	vreeze	Furcht
final	laatste	letzte
finite	eyndig	endlich
form	gedaante gestalte	Form
formality	omstandigheid	Mittel
formally	formelijk	auf formale Weise

ENGLISH	DUTCH	GERMAN
freedom	vryheid	Freiheit
fright	vervaartheid	Kleinmuth
future	die toekomende	Zukunft
grasp	begrijpen	begreifen
gratitude	dankbaarheid	Dankbarkeit
grief	beklagh	Gram
guess	gissen	muthmassen
hate	haat	Hass
hearsay	hooren zeggen	Hörensagen
honor	eere	Ehrliebe
hope	hope	Hoffnung
humility	nedrigheid	Demuth
hypocrites	geveysde	Heuchler
idea	begrip denkbeeld	Begriff Vorstellung
idea of God *idea dei*	idea van God	Vorstellung Gottes
imagination	verzieringe	Phantasie
immanent	inblijvend	immanente
immortality	onsterffelijkheid	Unsterblichkeit
important originat- ing	voornaam beginninde	vorzüglich veranlas- send
impulse	trek	Trieb
inclined	geneegen	geneigt
infallible	onfeylbaar	unfehlbar
infinite *infinitus* (I. def. 6)	oneyndig	unendlich
ingratitude	ondankbaarheid	Undankbarkeit
intelligible	verstandige	verständige
internal	in haar innerlijk	inner innerlich
intrinsically	door haar natuur	ihrer Natur nach
inviolable	onverbrekelijk	unverbrüchlich
jealousy	belgzucht jalousie	Eifersucht
jesting	boerterye	Scherz

ENGLISH	DUTCH	GERMAN
joy	blijdschap	Lust
knowable	kennelijk	erkennbar
knowledge	kennis weeten kundigheid kennisse	Erkenntniss Axiom Wissen
leave undone	nalaten te doen	unterlassen zu tun
legitimate	wettig	regelrecht
like (alike)	gelijk gelijkelijk	gleich
limited *terminari* I, 8	bepaald	bestimmt
love	liefde	Liebe
manifest	geeft te kenne	giebt kund
manifestation	vertooninge	Kundgebung
mischief	unheil	Unheil
mocking	bespotting	Spott
mode (manifestation) *Modus*	wijze wijzing modificatie	Modus
modification (*modificatio*)	wijzing	Modus
motion	beweging	Bewegung
multiplied	vermenigvuldight	multiplicirt
nature (essence) *natura* I, 7.	natuur	Natur Wesen
necessarily	noodzaakelijk	notwendigerweise
negative	ontkennend	verneinend
neighbor	evenmensch	Nebenmensch
noble mindedness	edelmoedigheid	Selbstachtung
non-being	niet zijn	Nichtsein
non-existent	niet zijnde	
oblong	lankwerpig	länglich
object *res*	voorwerp	Gegenstand
objectively	voorwerpelijk	objectiv
offensive	aanstotelijk	anstössig

ENGLISH	DUTCH	GERMAN
omnipotence	almachtigheid almogentheyd	Allmacht
omniscient	alwetend	allwissend
oneness	eenigheid	Einheid
operation	werking	Wirkung
opinion	waan	Meinung
oppress	prangen	drängen
oppression	pranging	Bedrängniss
originating	beginnende	beginnende
palpable	tastelijk	offenbar
particle	deeltje	Theilchen
passions	lijdinge (passien)	Leidenschaften
passive	lijdende	leidend
passivity	lijding	Leiden
perceive	gewaar worden	bemerken
perception	gewaarworden	Gewahrwerden
perfection	volmaaktheid	Vollkommenheit
perform	verrigten	verrichten
permanent	onvergankelijk	unvergänglich
persuaded	wijsgemakt	eingebildet
pleasure	lust	Lust
position	stelling	Lehre
positive	stellig	positiv
possible	gebeurlijk	zufällig
power	magt	Macht
powerful	krachtig	kräftig
praise	lof	Lob
predestination	praedestinatie	Vorherbestimmung
predestined	voorbepaalt	vorherbestimmt
predicated	gezeid	gestellt
predicate	gezeg	Prädicat
preëminent	voorgaand	disponirend
principal	voornaam	vorzüglich

ENGLISH	DUTCH	GERMAN
principle	beginsel	das Prinzip
principle	grondregel	Grundsatz
produce	voortbrengen	hervorbringen
product	gevrogte	Produkt
productive	daarstellend	darstellend
profit (profitableness)	nuttigheeden	Nutzen
properly	eigentlijk	eigentlich
proportion	gelijkmatigheid	Verhältniss
proud, to grow	verhovaardigen	hoffärtig werden
providence	voorzienigheid	Vorsehung
provider	voorzorger	Fürsorger
proximate	naaste	nächste
qualities	hoedanigheeden	Beschaffenheiten
reason	reede.	Vernunft
reasoning	redenen	Grund
regeneration	Wedergeboort	Wiedergeburt
regulated	gematigd	gewonnen
relation	betrekking	Verhältniss
religion	godsdienst	Religion
remorse	knaging	Gewissensbissen
remote	verder	entferntere
repentance	berouw	Reue
rest	ruste	Ruhe
righteous	rechtvaardig	gerecht
satisfy	voldoen	befriedigen
self-caused, self-existent.	door zig zelfs bestaande	durch sich bestehend
self-condemnation	strafbare needrigheid	Selbstverwerfung
self-contradictory	in zig selven strijdig	was sich selbst widerspricht
separately	afsonderlijk in het besonder.	abstrakt besonders
shame	beschaamtheid	Scham
shamelessness	onbeschaamtheid	Unverschämtheit

ENGLISH	DUTCH	GERMAN
signification	beteekening	Bezeichnung
single	eenvoudig	einfach
singleness	eenvoudigheid	Einfachheit
skeptic	Twijffelaar	Skeptiker
sorrow	droefheid	Unlust
soul	Ziel	Seele
species	geslagt	Geschlechtsbegriff
spirits	geesten	Geister
subject (adj.)	onderworpen	unterworfen
substance	zelfstandigheid	Substanz
substantial	zelfstandig	substantielle
surprise	verwondering	Verwunderung
terror	schrik	Schreck
thing	ding zaak	Ding
thought-entity	wezen van Reeden.	Gedankswesen Gedankending
transeunt	overgaand	Vorübergehend
transitory	vergankelijk	vergänglich
troubled, be	bedroeven	betrüben
true	waar	wahr
truth	waarheid	Wahrheit
unchangeable	onveranderlijk	unveränderlich
understand	verstaan	verstehen
understanding	verstand	Verstand
union	vereening	Vereinigung
unique	eenig	einzig
unite	vereenigen	vereinigen
unity	eenheid	Einheit
vacillation	wankelmoedigheid	Wankelmuth
vacuum	ydel	leeren Raum
valor	kloekmoedigheid	Herzhaftigkeit
vanity	ydelheid	Eitelkeit

ENGLISH	DUTCH	GERMAN
voluntarily	vrywillig	freiwillig
ward off	af weren	abwehren
will	wille	Wille
wrath	gramschap	Zorn
wretched	ellendig	elend

PHILOSOPHICAL CLASSICS

Published in The

Religion of Science Library

THE OPEN COURT PUBLISHING CO.

P. O. Drawer F   CHICAGO

Philosophical and Psychological Portrait Series

The portraits are printed on large paper (11x14), with tint and plate-mark, many of them are reproduced from rare paintings, engravings, or original photographs. They are suitable for framing and hanging in public and private libraries, laboratories, seminaries, recitation and lecture rooms, and will be of interest to all concerned in education and general culture. Complete details found in catalog of the Open Court. Sent on request.

The Psychological Series (25 portraits) on Imperial Japanese Vellum, $5.00 (24s.)

The Psychological Series (25 portraits) on plate paper, $3.75 (18s.)

The Philosophical Series (43 portraits) on plate paper, $6.25 (30s.) Not supplied on Vellum.

Both Series (68 portraits) on plate paper, $7.50 (35s.)
The higher prices in parentheses refer to foreign countries. Carriage prepaid. Single portraits, plate paper, 25 cents.
For subscribers who may prefer not to frame the portraits, a neat portfolio will be provided at a cost of $1.00 additional.

"I have received the first installment of portraits of philosophers, and am very much pleased with them."
—*Prof. David G. Ritchie, St. Andrews, Scotland.*

"I congratulate you on the magnificent character of the portraits, and I feel proud to have such adornments for my lecture room."
—*J. J. McNulty, Professor of Philosophy in the College of the City of New York.*

THE OPEN COURT PUBLISHING CO.

P. O. Drawer F   CHICAGO